How to knit

Debbie Bliss

C&B

COLLINS & BROWN

This book is for my mother, Mid, for all her encouragement, love and support

First published in Great Britain in 1999
by Collins & Brown Limited
London House
Great Eastern Wharf
Parkgate Road
London SW11 4NQ

1 3 5 7 9 8 6 4 2

British Library Cataloguing-in-Publication Data:
A catalogue record for this book
is available from the British Library.

ISBN 1 85585 674 3 (hardback edition)
ISBN 1 85585 696 4 (paperback edition)

Conceived, edited and designed by Collins & Brown Limited

 Editor: Kate Haxell
Designer: Sara Kidd
Photography: still life photography by Sandra Lane
            child and adult photography by Sandra Lousada
            details and cutouts by Sandra Lane, Sandra Lousada and Matthew Dickens

Reproduction by Hong Kong Graphic & Printing Ltd
Printed and bound in Hong Kong by Hong Kong Graphic & Printing Ltd

Contents

Introduction

EARLIER THIS YEAR I fulfilled a dream and opened a shop in London. This has given me the opportunity to meet and to talk to many knitters, particularly, to my great joy, many enthusiastic young or new ones, and I quickly found out that whatever our level of experience, we all had areas that we lacked confidence in. For some it was simply getting started, for others it was colour work such as Fair Isle and intarsia, while still others were worried about knitting lace effects. Many of the knitters I spoke to felt that they needed to look again at the finishing techniques they were using in order to produce a more professional-looking garment.

Through these conversations I devised a series of workshops to demystify these areas, and I have now been given the opportunity to publish them in book form. *How To Knit* is for anyone who wants to improve their knitting skills. If you have two left thumbs and have despaired of even being able to cast on a stitch, the *Beginner's Workshop* will get you started and the *Simple Stitch Patterns Workshop* will take you through the next steps. There is an *Aran*, a *Colour* and a *Lace Workshop*, each devoted to solving problems associated with that style of knitting, and a *Finishing Workshop* to help you over the last hurdles.

I have also included an *Entrelac Workshop* as I think that this style of knitting is seen as more complex that it really is, and a *Design Workshop* to get you started on your own projects. There are stitch libraries to introduce you to the huge range of patterns that exist and each workshop contains projects that I have specially designed to incorporate different techniques as you learn them.

This is my personal guide to knitting and I have tried to eliminate unnecessary and often confusing variations of some techniques and include instead my tried and tested favourites. I hope that the spirit of the original workshops comes over, with clear diagrams and simple explanations, and above all, I hope that this book will instill confidence in the reader.

All that is missing is the company of other enthusiasts, the gossip and cake, and endless cups of tea!

Debbie Bliss

CHAPTER ONE

Beginner's Workshop

I MUST HAVE LEARNED to knit when I was young but I have no childhood memories of a craft passed down by my mother – rather of the royal-blue cardigan that she took out of the bag every autumn, knitted a few more rows of, then packed away in the spring. I had outgrown it long before it was completed!

I rediscovered handknitting after completing a fashion and textiles course at art college. Excited by its possibilities, I started off by making three-dimensional objects – knitted plants such as cacti, daffodils and trailing fuschia – and then slowly moved into designing fashion handknits.

To begin with I found juggling colour, texture and pattern compiling (particularly the maths) rather daunting, but I soon found, as you will, that I gained in confidence and learned a little more every time I picked up yarn and a pair of needles.

In this first workshop you will learn, and then practice on two simple projects, the basic techniques that will be the foundation of all the projects you will tackle in the future. All you need is faith in your own ability.

Yarns

On these pages is a personal selection of yarns which I like to work with. They are all chosen from the Rowan range (see page 159 for stockists). I prefer to work with smooth, natural yarns that show up stitch detail well, but do visit your local knitting shop and look at the other yarns that are available.

Left *Wool*: this is hard-wearing with excellent insulating properties. Double Knitting (shown) is the most frequently used weight.

Left *Denim*: one of my favourite yarns; it fades just like your jeans with washing and wearing.

Right *Chenille*: this has a rich, velvety appearance but should be approached with care as it can look uneven when knitted up. Unravelling often makes the yarn 'bald' so it cannot be reused.

Right *Aran*: traditionally cream in colour and famously used in classic Aran designs, this yarn is now available in a range of shades.

Left *Tweed yarns*: these come in various weights and create subtle multi-coloured effects that can enliven classic designs.

Left *Cotton: this is excellent for showing up stitch detail and is non-allergic for most people. It is ideal for garments for babies and children.*

Right *Soft yarns: mohair and angora produce beautiful fabrics but the fibres mean that they are unsuitable for babies.*

Below *Chunky: thicker than Aran weight, this has the advantage of knitting up quickly.*

Equipment

The beginner only needs the most basic equipment to start with. Shown below are those things you really should have, plus a couple of extras that make a knitter's life easier.

Below *Scissors: small, sharp scissors are best. Do not be tempted to pull the yarn to break it as this will stretch it and can distort your knitting.*

Above *Tape measure: use a cloth tape measure to check your garment measurements.*

Above *Pins (left): used in checking tension (see page 13) and blocking out items (see page 156).*
Row counter (right): helpful for keeping track of rows worked, particularly when increasing and decreasing.

Below *Ruler: used for checking tension; a cloth tape is less accurate.*

Left Knitting *needles: made from plastic, aluminum or bamboo they come in varying lengths in pairs, double pointed in sets of four or as single circular needles. I have recently converted from plastic to bamboo, which are light and have a polished surface which lets the stitches glide along.*

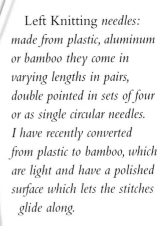

Right *Sewing needle: these need to have a large eye and a blunt point so that they do not split stitches when sewing up knitting.*
Stitch holder: used to secure stitches not in use. A safety pin can be used for a small number of stitches.

Working From A Pattern

Before starting any pattern, always read it through. This will give you an idea of how the design is structured and the techniques that are involved. Each pattern should include the following elements.

Measurements/Sizes

The instructions given can be in a range of sizes, with the smallest size printed first and the other sizes following in brackets. A pattern should quote the actual chest measurement, the length and the sleeve seams for each size. If you want to adjust the length of a garment, remember that this may alter the amounts of yarn that you will need.

Materials

This gives a list of materials required, including the amount of yarn, sizes of needles and any buttons or zips. The yarn amounts quoted are based on average requirements and are therefore approximate.

Abbreviations

Knitting instructions are normally given in an abbreviated form which saves valuable space. In this book the most commonly used abbreviations are listed on page 158 and additional abbreviations specific to a project are listed on the project page.

Garment Instructions

Before starting knitting, read the instructions carefully to understand the abbreviations used, how the design is structured and in which order each piece is worked. However, there may be some parts of the pattern that will only become clear when you are actually knitting it, so do not assume that you are being dense or that the pattern is wrong.

Patterns given in a range of sizes have the instructions for the smallest size printed first, followed by the other sizes in brackets. For example: 'Cast on 26(28, 30, 32) sts.'. To avoid confusion it is a good idea to go through the pattern and highlight all the figures for the size you are making. If the

pattern has metric and imperial measurements make sure that you do not mix the two up.

Asterisks or brackets are used to indicate the repetition of a sequence of stitches. For example: '*K3, p1; rep from * to end.'. This means, knit three stitches, then purl one stitch then repeat this sequence to the end of the row. It could also be written '[K3, p1] to end.'. Asterisks and brackets may be used together in a row. For example: '*K4, p1, [k1, p1] 3 times; rep from * to end.'. The part of the instruction in brackets indicates that these stitches only are to be repeated three times before returning to the instructions immediately after the asterisk.

When repeating anything, make sure that you are doing so the correct number of times. For example, '[K1, p1] twice.' means 4 stitches worked, but '*K1, p1; rep from * twice more.' means 6 stitches worked.

The phrase 'work straight' means continue without increasing or decreasing the number of stitches and keeping the established pattern correct.

When you put your knitting aside, always mark where you are on the pattern; it is better to be safe than sorry, especially if a complex stitch is involved.

If the figure 0 appears within an instruction, for example, 'K1(0:1:2) sts.' this means that for that particular size no stitches are worked at that point. Take special care if the sizes have been separated for a particular instruction. For example, suppose that the pattern states '**1st and 4th sizes only** Cast off 15(20) sts, work to end.'. For the 1st size, follow the instructions outside the round brackets, and for the 4th size follow those within them. For any other size, these instructions do not apply.

Some designs, particularly Aran styles, are made up of a combination of separate stitch panels which are often given as pattern panels at the beginning of the pattern. This is because the pattern cannot be set out in full for some reason, usually because the row repeat of each individual stitch pattern is not the same. I find it much easier to follow the patterns isolated in this way and to refer back to a specific panel if I have made a mistake or become confused. In the instructions for each piece there will be a few rows setting out the row on which to begin and the order in which the panel needs to be worked. On reaching the last row of the repeat of each panel start again from the first row, bearing in mind that you will be working different rows of panels at the same time.

With some designs, particularly lace, it can be difficult to keep the pattern when shaping. So, mark off your knitting where the repeat of the pattern starts at the beginning of the row and where it finishes at the end of the row. This will show you how many stitches need to be worked into the pattern. Work the stitches at the right-hand side of the knitting to match the end of the pattern repeat, and at the left-hand side to match the beginning of the pattern repeat.

Making Up

This will tell you how to join the knitted pieces together. Always follow the recommended sequence.

Knitting A Tension Swatch

No matter how excited you are about a new knitting project and how annoying it seems to have to spend time knitting up a tension swatch before you start, please do take the time, it won't be wasted.

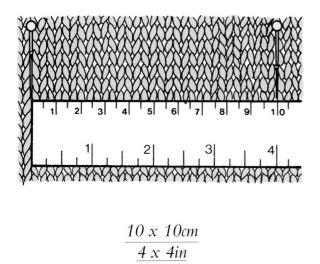

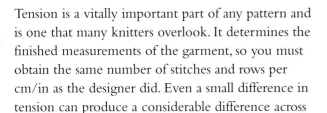

$$10 \times 10cm$$
$$4 \times 4in$$

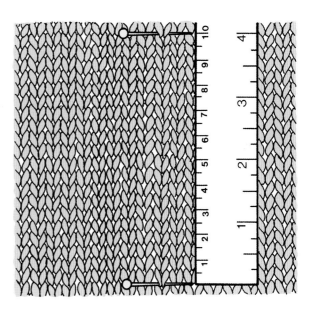

Tension is a vitally important part of any pattern and is one that many knitters overlook. It determines the finished measurements of the garment, so you must obtain the same number of stitches and rows per cm/in as the designer did. Even a small difference in tension can produce a considerable difference across the width of a design.

Use the same needles, yarn and stitch pattern as those to be used for the main work and knit a sample at least 12.5cm/5in square. Smooth out the finished piece on a flat surface, but do not stretch it.

To check the stitch tension, place a ruler horizontally on the sample and mark 10cm/4in across with pins. Count the number of stitches between the pins. To check the row tension, place a ruler vertically on the sample and mark 10cm/4in with pins. Count the number of rows between the pins. If the number of stitches and rows is greater then specified in the pattern, try again using larger needles; if it is less, try with smaller needles.

Holding The Yarn And Needles

Before casting on it is a good idea to get used to holding the yarn and needles.
Remember, they are bound to feel really awkward to begin with.

Holding The Needles

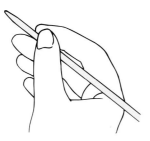

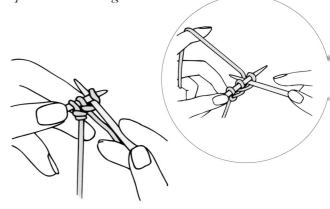

The right needle is held in the same way as a pencil. When casting on and working the first few rows the knitted piece passes over the hand, between the thumb and the index finger. As the work progresses, let the thumb slide under the knitted piece and hold the needle from below.

The left needle is held lightly over the top. If using the English method of knitting (main picture), the thumb and index finger control the tip of the needle. (If using the Continental method, see inset, control the tip with the thumb and middle finger.)

Holding The Yarn

There are several ways of winding the yarn around your fingers: these are the two I find easiest to use.

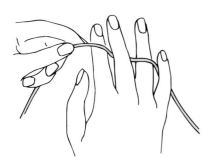

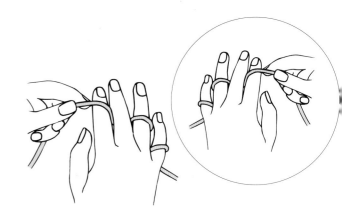

Method One

To hold the yarn in your right hand, pass it under your little finger, over your third finger, under your centre finger and over your index finger. Your index finger is used to pass the yarn around the tip of the needle. The tension on the yarn is controlled by gripping the yarn in the crook of the little finger.

Method Two

To hold the yarn in your right hand (left hand if using the Continental method, see inset), pass it under your little finger, then around this finger, over your third finger, under your centre finger and over your index finger. Your index finger is used to pass the yarn around the tip of the needle. The yarn circled around your little finger creates the necessary tension for even knitting.

Making A Slip Knot

A slip knot is the basis of all casting on techniques (see pages 16-17) and is therefore the starting point for almost everything you do in knitting.

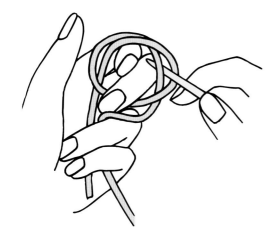

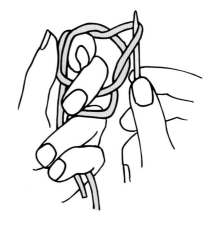

1 Wind the yarn around two fingers twice as shown. Insert a knitting needle through the first (front) strand and under the second (back) one.

2 Using the needle, pull the back strand through the front one to form a loop.

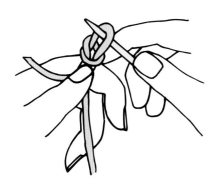

3 Holding the loose ends of the yarn with your left hand, pull the needle upwards, thus tightening the knot. Pull the ball end of the yarn again to tighten the knot further.

TIPS: GETTING STARTED

The yarn may be held in either the right or left hand; the two ways are referred to as the English and the Continental methods. Try holding the yarn in either of the ways shown opposite, though you may well develop a personal method. Ideally, ask a knitter to cast on a few stitches for you as it is easier to handle the yarn and needles with some stitches already cast on. I usually use the thumb method of casting on (see page 16) as it gives a neat, elastic edge that I like. The length of yarn between the cut end and the slip knot is used for making the stitches, so do allow enough; usually three to four times the finished width of the knitting. The cable method of casting on (see page 17) gives a firm, neat finish and is ideal for ribs. If you are a very tight knitter you may need to use a larger needle size to cast on with.

Casting On

Casting on is the term used for making a row of stitches to be used as a foundation for your knitting. There are several methods of casting on which produce different kinds of edges, but the two I prefer are the thumb method and the cable method.

Thumb Method

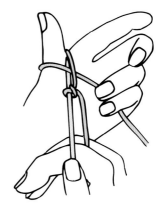

1 Make a slip knot 1m/39in (approximately enough yarn to cast on the back of a child's sweater) from the end of the yarn. Hold the needle in your right hand with the ball end of the yarn over your index finger. ★Wind the loose end of the yarn around your left thumb from front to back.

2 Insert the point of the needle under the first strand of yarn on your thumb.

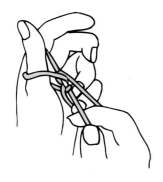

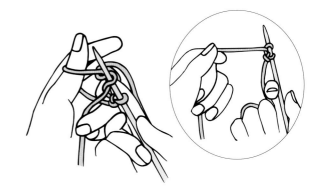

3 With your right index finger, take the ball end of the yarn over the point of the needle.

4 Pull a loop through to form the first stitch. Remove your left thumb from the yarn. Pull the loose end to secure the stitch (see inset). Repeat from ★ until the required number of stitches have been cast on.

Cable Method

1 This method of casting on requires two needles. Make a slip knot about 10cm/4in from the end of the yarn. Hold this needle in your left hand.

2 Insert the right-hand needle through the slip knot. Pass the yarn over the point of the right-hand needle.

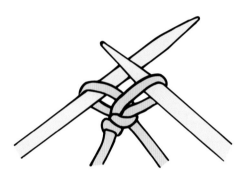

3 Pull a loop through the slip knot with the right-hand needle.

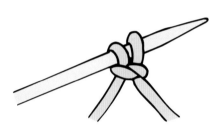

4 Place this loop on the left-hand needle. Gently pull the yarn to secure the stitch.

5 Insert the right-hand needle between the slip knot and the first stitch on the left-hand needle. Wind the yarn round the point of the right-hand needle.

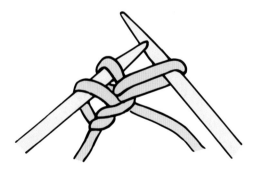

6 Draw a loop through, place this loop on the left-hand needle. Repeat steps 5 and 6 until the required number of stitches have been cast on.

The Basic Stitches

The knit and purl stitches form the basis of most knitted fabrics. The knit stitch is the easiest to learn and once you have mastered this, move on to the purl stitch which is slightly more complicated.

Knit Stitch

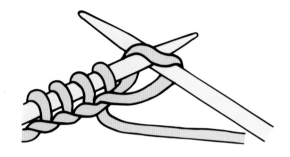

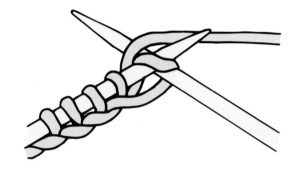

1 Hold the needle with the cast on stitches in your left hand, with the loose yarn at the back of the work. Insert the right-hand needle from left to right through the front of the first stitch on the left-hand needle.

2 Wind the yarn from left to right over the point of the right-hand needle.

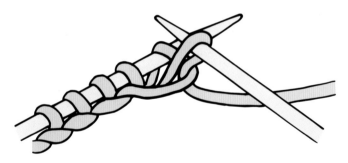

3 Draw the yarn through the stitch, thus forming a new stitch on the right-hand needle.

4 Slip the original stitch off the left-hand needle, keeping the new stitch on the right-hand needle.

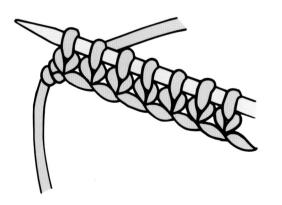

5 To knit a row, repeat steps 1 to 4 until all the stitches have been transferred from the left-hand needle to the right-hand needle. Turn the work, transferring the needle with the stitches on into your left hand to work the next row.

Purl Stitch

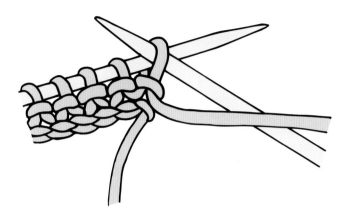

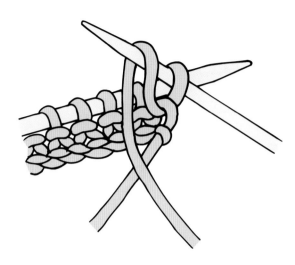

1 Hold the needle with the stitches on in your left hand, with the loose yarn at the front of the work. Insert the right-hand needle from right to left into the front of the first stitch on the left-hand needle.

2 Wind the yarn from right to left over the point of the right-hand needle.

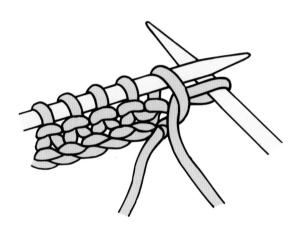

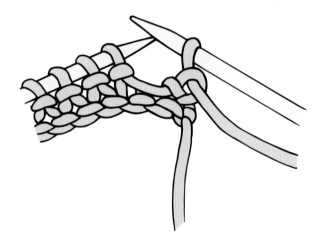

3 Draw the yarn through the stitch, thus forming a new stitch on the right-hand needle.

4 Slip the original stitch off the left-hand needle, keeping the new stitch on the right-hand needle.

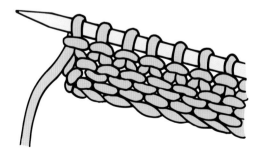

5 To purl a row, repeat steps 1 to 4 until all the stitches have been transferred from the left-hand needle to the right-hand needle. Turn the work, transferring the needle with the stitches on into your left hand to work the next row.

Increasing

The simplest method of increasing one stitch is to work into the front and back of the same stitch.

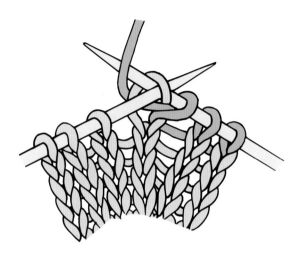

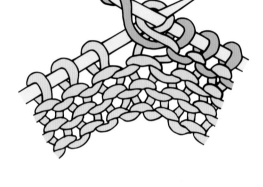

On a knit row, knit into the front of the stitch to be increased into, then before slipping it off the needle, place the right-hand needle behind the left-hand one and knit again into the back of it. Slip the original stitch off the left-hand needle.

On a purl row, purl into the front of the stitch to be increased into, then before slipping it off the needle, purl again into the back of it. Slip the original stitch off the left-hand needle.

Decreasing

The simplest method of decreasing one stitch is to work two stitches together.

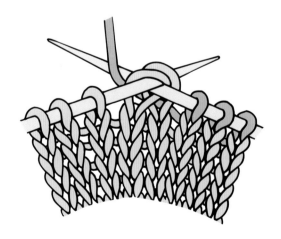

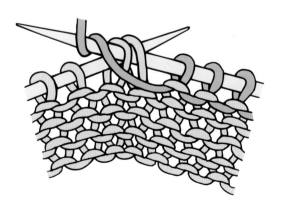

On a knit row, insert the right-hand needle from left to right through two stitches instead of one, then knit them together as one stitch. This is called knit two together (k2tog).

On a purl row, insert the right-hand needle from right to left through two stitches instead of one, then purl them together as one stitch. This is called purl two together (p2tog).

Casting Off

There is one simple, most commonly used method of securing stitches once you have finished a piece of knitting – casting off. The cast-off edge should always have the same 'give' or elasticity as the fabric and you should always cast off in the stitch used for the main fabric unless the pattern directs otherwise.

Knitwise

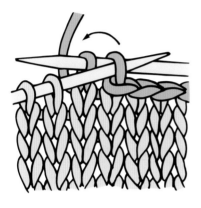

Purlwise

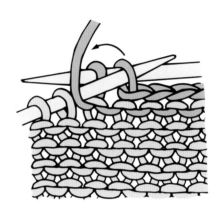

Knit two stitches. *Using the point of the left-hand needle lift the first stitch on the right-hand needle over the second then drop it off the needle. Knit the next stitch and repeat from * until all stitches have been worked off the left-hand needle and only one stitch remains on the right-hand needle. Cut the yarn (leaving enough to sew in the end, see page 68), thread the end through the stitch then slip it off the needle. Draw the yarn up firmly to fasten off.

Purl two stitches. *Using the point of the left-hand needle lift the first stitch on the right-hand needle over the second and drop it off the needle. Purl the next stitch and repeat from * until all the stitches have been worked off the left-hand needle and only one stitch remains on the right-hand needle. Secure the last stitch as described in casting off knitwise.

TIPS: CASTING OFF

The excitement of arriving at the last stage of your knitting can make you cast off without the same care that you have used in the rest the work. You should take into account the part of the garment you are working on. If it is a neckband you need to make sure that your cast-off edge is not too tight, preventing the neck from going over the wearer's head. If you are a tight knitter

you may need to cast off with a larger needle. Most neckbands or frontbands on a jacket or cardigan are worked in rib and should be cast off 'ribwise' by knitting the knit stitches and purling the purl stitches as you cast off along the row. Lace stitches should also be cast off in pattern, slipping, making stitches or decreasing as you go to make sure that the fabric doesn't widen or gather up.

Project 1: Garter-stitch Bag

This bag is knitted in the simplest stitch of all – garter stitch. As there is no shaping required you don't have to worry about increasing or decreasing and you can concentrate instead on producing a neat, even fabric and enjoying knitting your first project.

Materials

6 50g balls of Rowan DK Handknit Cotton.
Pair of 4mm (No 8/US 6) knitting needles.

Measurements

Approximately 33cm x 34cm/13in x 13½ in.

Tension

20 stitches and 38 rows to 10cm/4in square over garter st (every row k) on 4mm (No 8/US 6) needles.

Abbreviations

The instructions are written out in full for this project.

To Make

With 4mm (No 8/US 6) needles cast on 132 stitches.
1st row Knit to end.
This row forms garter stitch. Repeat this row until work measures 34cm/13½in from beginning.
Shape for Strap
Cast off knitwise 60 stitches at beginning of next 2 rows. 12 sts.
Continue on these stitches until strap measures approximately 75cm/29½in or required length. Cast off.

To Make Up (see also Finishing Workshop)

Fold bag in half widthwise and join side and bottom seam. Placing centre of cast-off edge of strap to side seam, sew strap in position.

Project 2: Stocking-stitch Sweater

This child's sweater is in stocking stitch with a garter-stitch hem which prevents the fabric rolling up. The front and the back are the same and no shaping is needed for the neck which has a slash opening. You will, however, be using the increase technique to shape the sleeves.

Materials

7(8:9:11:13) 50g balls of Rowan DK Handknit Cotton. Pair each of 3¾mm (No 9/US 4) and 4mm (No 8/US 6) knitting needles.

Measurements

To fit age	1-2	2-3	3-4	4-5	5-6	years
Actual chest	73	81	85	89	91	cm
measurement	28½	32	33½	35	36	in
Length	37	43	46	51	56	cm
	14½	17	18	20	22	in
Sleeve seam	20	22	24	27	30	cm
	8	8¾	9½	10½	11¾	in

Tension

20 stitches and 28 rows to 10cm/4in square over stocking stitch (1 row knit, 1 row purl) on 4mm (No 8/US 6) needles.

Abbreviations

The instructions are written out in full for this project.

Back

With 3¾mm (No 9/US 4) needles cast on 73(81:85:89:91) stitches. Knit 6 rows.
Change to 4mm (No 8/US 6) needles.
Beginning with a knit row, work in stocking stitch until the back measures 36(42:45:50:55)cm /14¼(16¾:17¾:19¾:21¾)in from beginning, ending with a knit row. Knit 5 rows. Cast off knitwise.

Front

Work as given for Back.

Sleeves

With 3¾mm (No 9/US 4) needles cast on 33(37:39:41:43) stitches. Knit 6 rows.
Change to 4mm (No 8/US 6) needles.
Beginning with a knit row, work 2 rows in stocking stitch.
Increase row Knit into front and back of first stitch, knit to last stitch, knit into front and back of last stitch.
Work 2 rows in stocking stitch.
Increase row Purl into front and back of first stitch, purl to last stitch, purl into front and back of last stitch.
Work 2 rows in stocking stitch.
Repeat last 6 rows 7(7:8:9:9) times more. 65(69:75:81:83) stitches. Continue straight for a few rows until sleeve measures 20(22:24:27:30)cm/8(8¾:9½:10½:11¾)in from beginning, ending with a purl row. Cast off loosely.

To Make Up (see also Finishing Workshop)

Lap the top garter stitch (every row knit) border of back over front and stitch through both thicknesses for approximately 7(9:10:11:12)cm/2¾(3½:4:4¼:4¾)in from each end for shoulders. Place markers 16(17:19:20:21)cm/6¼(6¾:7½:8:8¼)in down from shoulder seam at side edges of front and back. Sew in cast off edge of sleeves between markers. Join sleeve seams then side seams to top of garter stitch borders thus leaving small slits at side edges.

CHAPTER TWO

Simple Stitch Patterns Workshop

Nᴏᴡ ᴛʜᴀᴛ ʏᴏᴜ have successfully learned how to cast on and off, to knit and purl and to increase and decrease you are ready to tackle the next techniques – how to work a ribbed band, how to pick up stitches around a neck and how to work one of the most commonly used buttonholes.

As you will see from the swatches in the stitch library (pages 32-37), the most basic patterns can be very effective. Simple knit and purl combinations can produce subtle but beautiful textures, particularly if you use a good quality yarn that enhances the stitch. A classic pattern, such as moss stitch, can be used on a collar or to edge a jacket as an alternative to rib.

The projects you will undertake in this workshop are a garter-stitch and a moss-stitch cushion and a child's Guernsey-style sweater that incorporate all the techniques and stitches you learned in the *Beginner's Workshop* plus some new ones shown here.

Single And Double Rib

Rib is the most commonly used stitch for borders. It creates an elastic, flexible fabric which is particularly suitable for neckbands and cuffs as it stretches over the head and hands then springs back into shape.

Single Rib

The example below is worked over an even number of stitches, but it can be worked over any number.

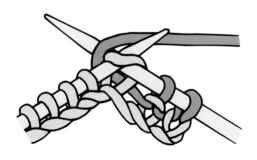

1 With the yarn at the back of the work, knit the first stitch.

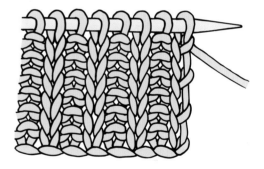

2 Bring the yarn forward to the front of the work between the needles then purl the next stitch.

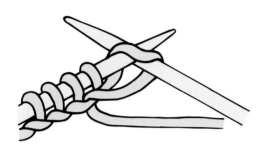

3 Take the yarn to the back of the work between the needles then knit the next stitch.

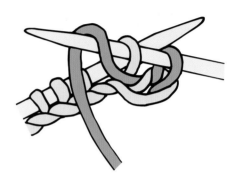

4 Repeat steps 2 and 3 until all stitches are on the right-hand needle, thus completing the 1st row.

On subsequent rows knit the stitches that were purled and purl the stitches that were knitted on the previous row. Over an odd number of stitches, single rib will begin and end with a knit stitch on the 1st row and with a purl stitch on the 2nd row. This would be written in the pattern instructions as follows (see page 158 for abbreviations):

1st row: K1, *p1, k1; rep from * to end.
2nd row: P1, *k1, p1; rep from * to end.
Rep these 2 rows.

Double Rib

Double rib can only be worked over an even number of stitches divisible by 4 or 4 plus 2 stitches. The example below is worked over a number divisible by 4 plus 2.

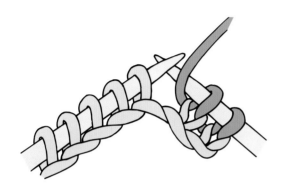

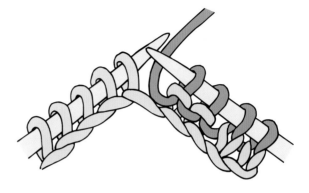

1 With the yarn at the back of the work, knit the first two stitches. Bring the yarn forward to the front of the work between the needles.

2 Purl the next two stitches and take the yarn to the back of the work between the needles.

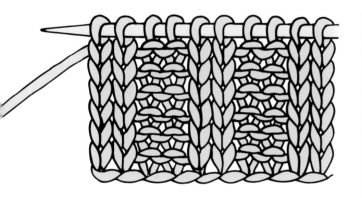

3 Continue in this way until all the stitches are transferred to the right-hand needle, thus completing the 1st row.

On subsequent rows purl the stitches that were knitted and knit the stitches that were purled on the previous row. If the 1st row begins and ends with two knit stitches, therefore the 2nd row will begin and end with two purl stitches.
This would be written in the instructions as follows:
1st row: K2, *p2, k2; rep from * to end.
2nd row: P2, *k2, p2; rep from * to end.
Rep these 2 rows.

TIPS: RIBBING

It is very important to maintain a constant tension when working a rib as the action of the yarn as it passes backwards and forwards between the knit and purl stitches can loosen up the work. For this reason ribs are usually knitted on needles two sizes smaller than those used for the main fabric of the garment.

If the main garment is worked in either a colour pattern or a stitch pattern that will pull in the work more tightly than usual, it is even more crucial that the rib is not loose as the contrast between the limp, non-elastic welt and the more dense fabric of the rest of the garment will create a fluted effect.

The decision as to whether to use a single or double rib on welts is down to both the style of the garment and to personal choice. A single rib will pull the welt in more than a double, and a double rib can be effective when worked into cables in an Aran-style design

Picking Up Stitches

An edging or a border can be added to the main body of the knitting by sewing it on (see pages 150-152) or by picking up stitches, usually referred to as 'pick up and knit' or 'knit up'.

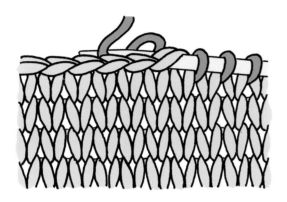 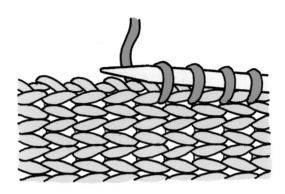

To pick up along a cast-on/cast-off edge (for instance along cast-off stitches at back neck), have the right side of the work facing you and insert the point of the right-hand needle from front to back under both loops of the cast-on or cast-off edge of the first stitch, wind the yarn round the point of the needle and draw a loop through, as though knitting a stitch, to form a new stitch on the needle. Continue in this way along the edge for as many stitches as required.

To pick up along a side edge (for instance along the straight front edge of jacket), have the right side of the work facing you and insert the point of the right-hand needle from front to back between the first and second stitch of the first row (working one whole stitch in from the edge). Wind the yarn round the point of the needle and draw a loop through, as though knitting a stitch, to form a new stitch on the needle. Continue in this way along the edge for as many stitches as required. If the yarn is very thick, work through the centre of the edge stitch, thus taking in only half a stitch and reducing the bulk.

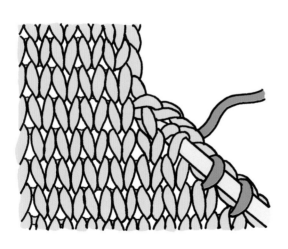

To pick up stitches along a shaped edge (for instance along a V-neck), use the above techniques to pick up the stitches around the straight side of the neck. On the shaped part of the neck insert the needle into the stitches one row below the decreasing and not between the stitches as this may form a hole. Draw through a loop to make a stitch as before.

Making A Stitch (m1)

This form of increasing involves working into the strand between two stitches. By working into the back of the 'lifted' stitch you twist the strand, preventing the hole that would be formed otherwise.

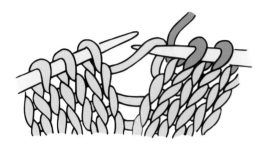

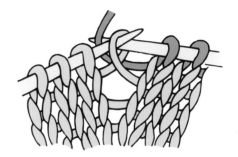

1 Insert the right-hand needle from front to back under the horizontal strand which runs between the stitch just worked on the right-hand needle and the next stitch on the left-hand needle.

2 Place the strand from back to front over the left-hand needle and knit or purl through the back of it.

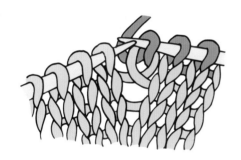

3 A completely new stitch is formed on the right-hand needle. Drop the strand off the left-hand needle.

Cast-off Buttonhole

A garment can be spoiled by badly worked buttonholes so it is important to work them correctly for a neat finish. Choosing the perfect buttons makes the task of completing the design more fun.

This buttonhole is worked over two rows and comprises stitches cast off in one row and cast on again in the next. The number of cast-off stitches depends on the button size and thickness of yarn.

On a right side row, work to the start of the button-hole, cast off the required number of stitches, then work to the end of the row. On the next row, work to the cast-off stitches, turn and cast on the same number of stitches using the cable method (see page 17), turn and work to the end.

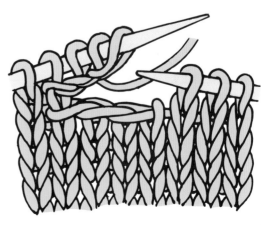

Simple Stitch Patterns Stitch Library

Our first stitch library is comprised of twenty-five patterns that are very easy to work. It is well worth trying them in a variety of weights and types of yarn so that you can see how they alter accordingly. For instance, a subtle stitch such as Simple Seed Stitch or Diamond Panels may be enhanced by using a good quality cotton yarn that will create better stitch detail than a wool or wool combination. Darker shades and tweeds or textured yarns may obscure some of these simple stitch patterns.

Garter Stitch

Any number of stitches.
1st row Knit to end.
Rep this row.

Stocking Stitch

Any number of stitches.
1st row (right side) Knit to end.
2nd row Purl to end.
Rep these 2 rows.

Moss Stitch

Multiple of 2 sts + 1 st.
1st row K1, [p1, k1] to end.
Rep this row.

Single Rib

1st row (right side) K1, [p1, k1] to end.
2nd row P1, [k1, p1] to end.
Rep these 2 rows.

Double Rib

Multiple of 4 sts + 2 sts.
1st row (right side) K2, [p2, k2] to end.
2nd row P2, [k2, p2] to end.
Rep these 2 rows.

Reverse Stocking Stitch

Any number of stitches.
Note: Work as stocking stitch with purl as right side.
1st row (right side) Purl to end.

2nd row Knit to end.

Rep these 2 rows.

Double Moss Stitch

Multiple of 2 sts + 1 st.

1st row (right side) K1, [p1, k1] to end.

2nd row P1, [k1, p1] to end.

3rd row P1, [k1, p1] to end.

4th row K1, [p1, k1] to end.

Rep these 4 rows.

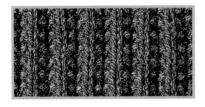

Moss Rib

Multiple of 4 sts + 1 sts.

1st row (right side) K2, [p1, k3] to last 3 sts, p1, k2.

2nd row P1, [k3, p1] to end.

Rep these 2 rows.

Woven Stitch

Multiple of 4 sts + 2 sts.

1st row (right side) Knit to end.

2nd row Purl to end.

3rd row K2, [p2, k2] to end.

4th row P2, [k2, p2] to end.

5th row Knit to end.

6th row Purl to end.

7th row P2, [k2, p2] to end.

8th row K2, [p2, k2] to end.

Rep these 8 rows.

Diamond Panels

Multiple of 8 sts + 1 st.

1st row (right side) Knit to end.

2nd row K1, [p7, k1] to end.

3rd row K4, [p1, k7] to last 5 sts, p1, k4.

4th row K1, [p2, k1, p1, k1, p2, k1] to end.

5th row K2, ★[p1, k1] twice, p1, k3; rep from ★ to last 7 sts, [p1, k1] twice, p1, k2.

6th row As 4th row.

7th row As 3rd row.

8th row As 2nd row.

Rep these 8 rows.

Lattice Stitch

Multiple of 6 sts + 1 st.

1st row (right side) K3, p1, [k5, p1] to last 3 sts, k3.

2nd row P2, k1, p1, k1, [p3, k1, p1, k1] to last 2 sts, p2.

3rd row K1, p1, [k3, p1, k1, p1] to last 5 sts, k3, p1, k1.

4th row K1, [p5, k1] to end.

5th row As 3rd row.

6th row As 2nd row.

Rep these 6 rows.

Simple Seed Stitch

Multiple of 4 sts + 1 st.
1st row (right side) P1, [k3, p1] to end.
2nd row Purl to end.
3rd row Knit to end.
4th row Purl to end.
5th row K2, p1, [k3, p1] to last 2 sts, k2.
6th to 8th rows As 2nd to 4th rows.
Rep these 8 rows.

Caterpillar Stitch

Multiple of 8 sts + 6 sts.
1st row (right side) K4, p2, [k6, p2] to end.
2nd row P1, k2, [p6, k2] to last 3 sts, p3.
3rd row K2, p2, [k6, p2] to last 2 sts, k2.
4th row P3, k2, [p6, k2] to last st, p1.
5th row P2, [k6, p2] to last 4 sts, k4.
6th row Purl to end.
Rep these 6 rows.

Double Parallelogram Stitch

Multiple of 10 sts.
1st row (right side) [P5, k5] to end.
2nd row K1, [p5, k5] to last 9 sts, p5, k4.
3rd row P3, [k5, p5] to last 7 sts, k5, p2.
4th row K3, [p5, k5] to last 7 sts, p5, k2.
5th row P1, [k5, p5] to last 9 sts, k5, p4.
6th row P4, [k5, p5] to last 6 sts, k5, p1.
7th row K2, [p5, k5] to last 8 sts, p5, k3.
8th row P2, [k5, p5] to last 8 sts, k5, p3.
9th row K4, [p5, k5] to last 6 sts, p5, k1.
10th row [K5, p5] to end.
Rep these 10 rows.

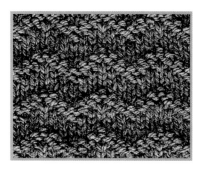

Reverse Stocking-stitch Chevrons

Multiple of 6 sts + 5 sts.
1st row (right side) K5, [p1, k5] to end.
2nd row K1, [p3, k3] to last 4 sts, p3, k1.
3rd row P2, [k1, p2] to end.
4th row P1, [k3, p3] to last 4 sts, k3, p1.
5th row K2, [p1, k5] to last 3 sts, p1, k2.
6th row Purl to end.
Rep these 6 rows.

Little Arrows

Multiple of 8 sts + 1 st.
1st row (right side) K1, [p1, k5, p1, k1] to end.
2nd row P1, [k2, p3, k2, p1] to end.
3rd row K2, p2, k1, p2, [k3, p2, k1, p2] to last 2 sts, k2.
4th row P3, k1, p1, k1, [p5, k1, p1, k1] to last 3 sts, p3.
Rep these 4 rows.

Diagonal Garter Ribs

Multiple of 5 sts + 2 sts.
1st and every alt row (right side) Knit to end.
2nd row [P2, k3] to last 2 sts, p2.
4th row K1, [p2, k3] to last st, p1.
6th row K2, [p2, k3] to end.
8th row [K3, p2] to last 2 sts, k2.
10th row P1, [k3, p2] to last st, k1.
Rep these 10 rows.

Chequerboard

Multiple of 8 sts + 4 sts.
1st row K4, [p4, k4] to end.
2nd row P4, [k4, p4] to end.
3rd row As 1st row
4th rows As 2nd row.
5th row P4, [k4, p4] to end.
6th row K4, [p4, k4] to end.
7th and 8th rows As 5th and 6th rows
Rep these 8 rows.

Chevron Rib

Multiple of 12 sts + 1 st.
1st row (right side) P2, k2, p2, k1, p2, k2, [p3, k2, p2, k1, p2, k2] to last 2 sts, p2.
2nd row K1, [p2, k2, p3, k2, p2, k1] to end.
3rd row K2, p2, k2, p1, k2, p2, [k3, p2, k2, p1, k2, p2] to last 2 sts, k2.
4th row P1, [k2, p2, k3, p2, k2, p1] to end.
Rep these 4 rows.

Moss-stitch Zigzag

Multiple of 9 sts.

1st row (right side) ★[K1, p1] twice, k4, p1; rep from ★ to end.
2nd row ★P4, [k1, p1] twice, k1; rep from ★ to end.
3rd row [K1, p1] 3 times, ★k4, [p1, k1] twice, p1; rep from ★ to last 3 sts, k3.
4th row P2, ★[k1, p1] twice, k1, p4; rep from ★ to last 7 sts, [k1, p1] twice, k1, p2.
5th row K3, ★[p1, k1] twice, p1, k4; rep from ★ to last 6 sts, [p1, k1] 3 times.
6th row ★ [K1, p1] twice, k1, p4; rep from ★ to end.
7th row As 5th row.
8th row As 4th row.
9th row As 3rd row.
10th row As 2nd row.
Rep these 10 rows.

Moss-stitch Triangles

Multiple of 8 sts.

1st row (right side) [P1, k7] to end.
2nd row P6, [k1, p7] to last 2 sts, k1, p1.
3rd row [P1, k1, p1, k5] to end.
4th row P4, [k1, p1, k1, p5] to last 4 sts, [k1, p1] twice.
5th row ★[P1, k1] twice, p1, k3; rep from ★ to end.
6th row P2, ★[k1, p1] twice, k1, p3; rep from ★ to last 6 sts, [k1, p1] 3 times.
7th row ★P1, k1; rep from ★ to end.

8th row As 6th row.
9th row As 5th row.
10th row As 4th row.
11th row As 3rd row.
12th row As 2nd row.
Rep these 12 rows.

Anchor

Worked over 17 sts on background of st st.

1st row (right side) P3, k11, p3.
2nd row K1, p1, [k1, p5] twice, k1, p1, k1.
3rd row P3, k4, p1, k1, p1, k4, p3.
4th row K1, p1, k1, p3, [k1, p1] twice, k1, p3, k1, p1, k1.
5th row P3, k2, p1, k5, p1, k2, p3.
6th row [K1, p1] twice, [k1, p3] twice, [k1, p1] twice, k1.
7th row P3, k1, p1, k7, p1, k1, p3.
8th row As 2nd row.
9th and 10th rows As 1st and 2nd rows.
11th row As 1st row.
12th row K1, p1, k1, p3, k5, p3, k1, p1, k1.
13th row P3, k3, p5, k3, p3.
14th row As 12th row.
15th to 18th rows Rep 1st and 2nd rows twice.
19th row As 3rd row.
20th row K1, p1, [k1, p3] 3 times, k1, p1, k1.
21st row As 3rd row.
22nd row As 2nd row.
23rd row As 1st row.
24th row K1, p1, k1, p11, k1, p1, k1.
Rep these 24 rows.

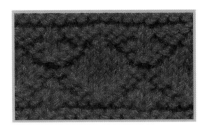

Ridge And Diamond Stripes

Multiple of 8 sts + 7 sts.
1st row (right side) P7, [k1, p7] to end.
2nd row K3, p1, [k2, p3, k2, p1] to last 3 sts, k3.
3rd row P2, k3, [p2, k1, p2, k3] to last 2 sts, p2.
4th row K1, p5, [k3, p5] to last st, k1.
5th row K7, [p1, k7] to end.
6th row As 4th row.
7th row As 3rd row.
8th row As 2nd row.
9th row As 1st row.
10th, 11th and 12th rows Purl to end.
Rep these 12 rows.

Tree Of Life

Worked over 23 sts on background of st st.
1st row (right side) P4, k7, p1, k7, p4.
2nd row K1, p2, k1, p6, k1, p1, k1, p6, k1, p2, k1.
3rd row P4, k5, p1, k3, p1, k5, p4.
4th row [K1, p2, k1, p4, k1, p2] twice, k1.
5th row P4, k3, p1, k2, p1, k1, p1, k2, p1, k3, p4.
6th row [K1, p2] 3 times, k1, p3, [k1, p2] 3 times, k1.
7th row P4, k1, [p1, k2] 4 times, p1, k1, p4.
8th row K1, p2, k1, p3, k1, p2, k1, p1, k1, p2, k1, p3, k1, p2, k1.

9th row P4, [k2, p1] twice, k3, [p1, k2] twice, p4.
10th row As 4th row.
11th row As 5th row.
12th row K1, p2, k1, p5, k1, p3, k1, p5, k1, p2, k1.
13th row P4, k4, [p1, k2] twice, p1, k4, p4.
14th row As 2nd row.
15th row As 3rd row.
16th row K1, p2, k1, [p7, k1] twice, p2, k1.
17th row P4, k6, p1, k1, p1, k6, p4.
18th row K1, p2, k1, p15, k1, p2, k1.
19th row As 1st row.
20th row As 18th row.
Rep these 20 rows.

Flying Wedge

Worked over 18 sts on background of st st.
1st row (wrong side) P18.
2nd row K11, p1, k6.
3rd row P7, k1, p10.
4th row K9, p1, k1, p1, k6.
5th row P7, k1, p1, k1, p8.
6th row K7, [p1, k1] twice, p1, k6.
7th row P7, [k1, p1] 5 times, k1.
8th row [K1, p1] 6 times, k6.
9th row P5, [k1, p1] 5 times, k1, p2.
10th row K3, [p1, k1] 5 times, p1, k4.
11th row P3, [k1, p1] 5 times, k1, p4.
12th row K5, [p1, k1] 5 times, p1, k2.
13th row [P1, k1] 6 times, p6.
14th row K7, [p1, k1] 5 times, p1.
15th row P7, [k1, p1] twice, k1, p6.
16th row K7, p1, k1, p1, k8.
17th row P9, k1, p1, k1, p6.
18th row K7, p1, k10.
19th row P11, k1, p6.
20th row K18.
Rep these 20 rows.

Project 3: Garter- and Moss-stitch Cushions

Both of these cushions are knitted in a pure wool yarn with a tweed effect. The button detailing, different on each, serves to enhance the simplicity of the design.

For Each Cushion

Materials

5 50g balls of Rowan DK Tweed.
Pair of 4mm (No 8/US 6) knitting needles.
6 buttons.
50cm/20in square cushion pad.

Measurements

Approximately 50cm/20in square.

Abbreviations

See page 158.

Garter-stitch Cushion

Tension

20 sts and 40 rows to 10cm/4in square over garter st on 4mm (No 8/US 6 needles).

Back

With 4mm (No 8/US 6) needles cast on 101 sts.
1st row K.
This row forms garter st. Work in garter st until back measures 50cm/20in from beg. Mark each end of last row. Garter st a further 5cm/2in.
1st buttonhole row K14, [cast off 3 sts, k11 including st used in casting off] 5 times, cast off 3 sts, k to end.
2nd buttonhole row K14, [cast on 3 sts, k11] 5 times, cast on 3 sts, k to end.
Work a further 3cm/1¼ in in garter st. Cast off.

Front

With 4mm (No 8/US 6) needles cast on 101 sts.
Work in garter st as given for Back until front measures 50cm/20in from beg. Cast off.

To Make Up (see also Finishing Workshop)

Placing cast on edge of back and cast on edge of front together, and cast off edge of front in line with markers on back, join the three sides together. Fold over remainder of back and sew on buttons on front to correspond with buttonholes on back.

Moss-stitch Cushion

Tension

21 sts and 36 rows to 10cm/4in square over moss st on 4mm (No 8/US 6) needles.

Front

With 4mm (No 8/US 6) needles cast on 105 sts.
1st row K1, [p1, k1] to end.
This row forms moss st. Work in moss st until front measures 50cm/20in from beg.
1st buttonhole row Moss st 16, [cast off 3 sts, moss st 11 including st used in casting off] 5 times, cast off 3 sts, moss st to end.
2nd buttonhole row Moss st 16, [cast on 3 sts, moss st 11] 5 times, cast on 3 sts, moss st to end.
Work a further 3cm/1in in moss st. Cast off.

Back

With 4mm (No 8/US 6) needles cast on 105 sts.
1st row K1, [p1, k1] to end.
Rep this row until back measures 53cm/21in from beg. Cast off.

To Make Up (see also Finishing Workshop)

Placing cast on edge of back and cast on edge of front together, join the three sides together, leaving buttonhole edge free. Sew buttons on inside of back to correspond with buttonholes on front.

Project 4: Child's Guernsey

This simple design, based on a traditional fisherman style, is worked mainly in stocking stitch with yoke and shoulder details. The ribs begin or end with some stocking stitch rows that roll back onto the fabric.

Materials

7(8:9) 50g balls of Rowan Designer DK Wool.
Pair each of 3¼mm (No 10/US 3) and 4mm
(No 8/US 6) knitting needles.

Measurements

To fit age	3-4	4-6	6-8 years	
Actual chest				
measurement	81	86	96	cm
	32	34	37¾	in
Length	42	48	53	cm
	16½	19	21	in
Sleeve seam	30	33	36	cm
	11¾·	13	14	in

Tension

24 sts and 32 rows to 10cm/4in square over st st (1 row
k, 1 row p) on 4mm (No 8/US 6) needles.

Abbreviations

See page 158.

Back

With 3¼mm (No 10/US 3) needles cast on 94 (102:114)
sts. Beg with a k row, work 6 rows in st st.

1st rib row (right side) K2, [p2, k2] to end.
2nd rib row P2, [k2, p2] to end.
Work 1st, 2nd and 1st rib row again.
Inc row Rib 22(50: 56), [inc in next st, rib 23(51:57)]
3(1:1) times. 97(103:115) sts.
Change to 4mm (No 8/US 6) needles.
Beg with a k row, work in st st until back measures
23(28:33)cm/9(11:13)in from beg, ending with a right
side row.
Work in yoke pattern as follows:
1st row K.
2nd and 3rd rows P.
4th and 5th rows K.
6th and 7th rows P.
8th row K3, [p1, k5] to last 4 sts, p1, k3.
9th row P2, [k1, p1, k1, p3] to last 5 sts, k1, p1, k1, p2.
10th row K1, [p1, k3, p1, k1] to end.
11th row K1, [p5, k1] to end.
12th row As 10th row.
13th row As 9th row.
14th row As 8th row.
15th row P.
16th row K.
17th to 23rd rows As 1st to 7th rows.
24th row K.
25th to 30th rows P1, [k1, p1] to end.
31st row P.
32nd row K.
These 32 rows form yoke patt. Rep them once more. ★★
Continue in garter stitch (every row k) until back
measures 42(48:53)cm/16½(19:21)in from beg, ending
with a wrong side row. Cast off. Mark 29th(31st:36th) sts
from each side edge for shoulders.

Front

Work as given for back to ★★.
Shape Neck
Next row K36(38:43), turn.
Work in garter stitch on this set of sts only. Dec one st
(by working 2 sts tog) at neck edge on next 7 rows.
29(31:36) sts. Cont straight until front measures same as
back to cast off edge, ending with a wrong side row.
Cast off.
With wrong side facing, slip centre 25(27:29) sts onto a
holder, rejoin yarn to rem sts and k to end. Complete as
given for first side of neck.

Sleeves

With 3¼mm (No 10/US 3) needles cast on 46(46:50) sts. Beg with a k row, work 6 rows in st st. Rep the 2 rows of rib as given for back 5 times, then work 1st row again.
Inc row Rib 2(2:4), inc in next st, [rib 6, inc in next st] to last 1(1:3) sts, rib to end. 53(53:57) sts.
Change to 4mm (No 8/US 6) needles.
Beg with a k row, work 4 rows in st st.
Inc row K twice in first st, k to last st, k twice in last st. Work 3 rows in st st. Rep the last 4 rows 8(11:12) times more, then work the inc row again. 73(79:85) sts. Work 4(6:8) rows straight.
Now work the 32 rows of yoke patt as given for back once, then work 1st to 16th rows again. Cast off loosely.

Neckband

Join right shoulder seam.

With 3¼mm (No 10/US 3) needles and right side facing, pick up and k16(18:18) sts down left front neck edge, k25(27:29) sts from centre, pick up and k15(17:17) sts up right front neck edge and 38(40:42) sts between markers at centre back neck, turn. 94(102:106) sts. K 1 row. P 2 rows. Beg with 1st row, work 12 rows in rib as given for back welt. Beg with a k row, work 4 rows in st st. Cast off loosely knitwise.

To Make Up (see also Finishing Workshop)

Join left shoulder and neckband seam, reversing seam on stocking stitch section of neckband. Mark side edges of back and front approximately 16(17:18)cm/6¼(6¾:7)in down from shoulders for armholes. Sew cast off edge of sleeves between markers. Join side and sleeve seams, reversing seams on 6 rows of stocking stitch at lower edges of welt and cuffs.

CHAPTER THREE

Aran Workshop

IN THIS WORKSHOP you will discover how to create intricate textured fabrics using combinations of cables and bobbles. If you are a new knitter this may well be the point at which you discover the endless possibilities that the craft can offer you, because the effect you now will be creating is completely unique to knitting. Don't, however, be put off by the often quite complicated look of Aran knitting: it really isn't terribly difficult to master. Work through the *Techniques* pages first, then a methodical approach will see you through the projects.

Traditionally Aran sweaters were hard-wearing garments made weatherproof by the dense fabric created by the cabling. The stitch patterns were worked in vertical panels, often with the addition of decorative bobbles.

As a knitwear designer nothing gives me more pleasure than taking these classic elements and giving them a contemporary twist, or playing around with separate cable panels until I find the perfect combination.

The first project is a simple child's sweater that encourages you to work cables that cross at the front and the back. The throw uses a slightly more complex cable but there is no shaping to do. The third project is a child's coat which introduces bobbles and twisted stitches.

Basic Cables

Cables are achieved by crossing one group of stitches over another. The number of stitches that are crossed can vary to make larger and smaller cables, and the number of rows between each cross can also vary. Once the basic cable technique has been mastered it can be used to reproduce many pattern variations. Here the cable panel consists of four stitches in stocking stitch worked on a reverse stocking-stitch background.

Cable 4 Back (C4B)

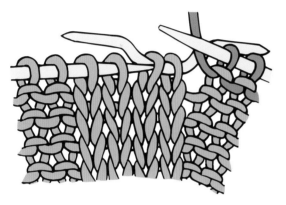

1 On a right side row, work to the position of the cable panel then slip the next two stitches onto the cable needle.

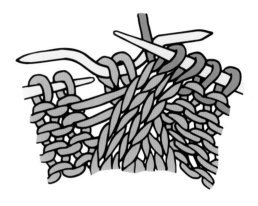

2 With the stitches on the cable needle held at the back of the work, knit the next two stitches from the left-handle needle.

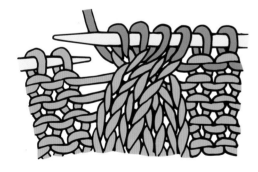

3 Now knit the two stitches from the cable needle to produce a cable that crosses to the right.

TIPS: CABLES
Cables are worked with the help of a small double-pointed needle called a cable needle (see inset picture). Some cable needles have a kink in them which is useful as it helps prevent the stitches you are holding from slipping off.
Cables are usually worked on a reverse stocking-stitch background so that the actual cable stands out clearly, though there are exceptions to this. The stitches making up the cable itself can be purled rather than knitted.

Cable 4 Front (C4F)

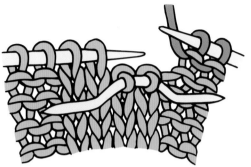

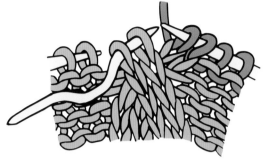

1 On a right side row, work to the position of the cable panel then slip the next two stitches onto the cable needle, leaving it at the front of the work.

2 Working behind the cable needle, knit the next two stitches from the left-hand needle.

3 Now knit the two stitches from the cable needle to produce a cable that crosses to the left.

Right *This detail from Project 5: Simple Cable Sweater (see page 58) clearly shows the difference between back cross (to the right) and front cross (to the left) cables. On an Aran with a centre panel such cables are often crossed at the back on one side of the panel and at the front on the other side to produce a pleasing symmetrical effect.*

Travelling Cables

Rather than simply crossing over itself, here the cable consists of two stitches in stocking stitch that travel diagonally over a reverse stocking-stitch background.

Cross 3 Right (Cr3R)

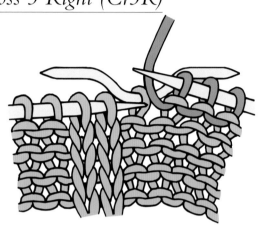

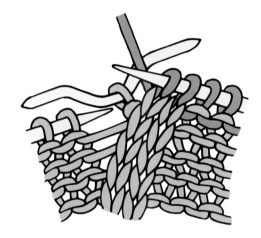

1 Work to one stitch before the two knit stitches. Slip the next stitch onto a cable needle and leave it at the back of the work.

2 Knit the next two stitches from the left-hand needle.

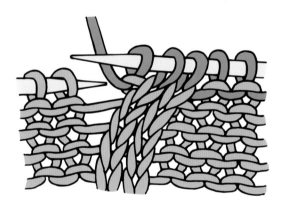

3 Now purl the stitch from the cable needle to produce a cable that travels to the right.

Right *This cable which is used in Project 7: Child's Aran Coat (see page 62) is relatively easy to knit. It uses twisted stitches which help to make the single stitches stand out more clearly against the background.*

Cross 3 Left (Cr3L)

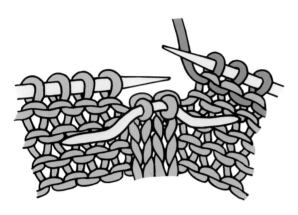

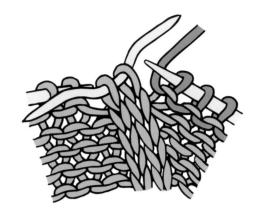

1 Work to the two knit stitches. Slip these two stitches onto a cable needle and leave them at the front of the work.

2 Purl the next stitch from the left-hand needle.

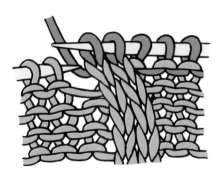

3 Knit the two stitches from the cable needle to produce a cable that travels to the left.

Knit/Purl Through Back Of Stitch

Knitting or purling into the back of a loop twists the stitch, making it firmer and more distinct. This technique is often combined with cable stitches to make the resulting patterns more defined.

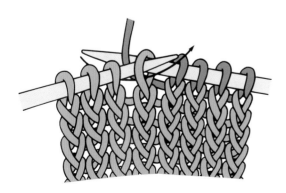

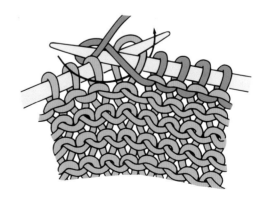

Knit into the back loop of the stitch instead of the front. This is called knit through back loop (k1 tbl).

Purl into the back loop of the stitch instead of the front. This is called purl through back loop (p1 tbl).

Twisting Stitches

Here the knit stitch is 'twisted' over reverse stocking-stitch fabric. This means that the stitches are crossed over one another but a cable needle is not required.

Twist 2 Back (T2B)

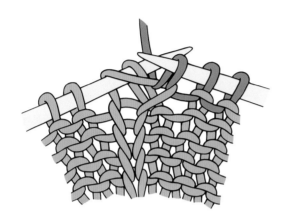

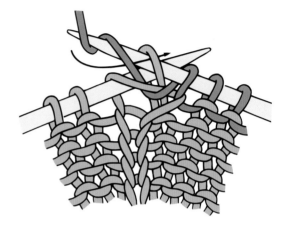

1 Work to one stitch before the knit stitch. Miss the first stitch, then knit the second (the knit) stitch through the front of the loop.

2 Without slipping the worked stitch off the needle, bring the yarn to the front and purl the missed stitch through the front of the loop, then slip both stitches off the left-hand needle together.

Twist 2 Front (T2F)

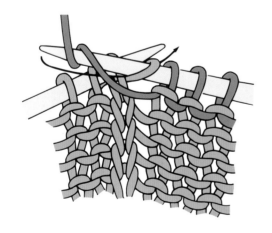

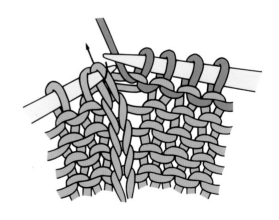

1 Work to the knit stitch. Miss the first (the knit) stitch, then purl the second stitch through the back of the loop, working behind the first stitch.

2 Without slipping the worked stitch off the needle, take the yarn back and knit the missed stitch through front of the loop, then slip both stitches off the left-hand needle together.

Four-stitch Bobble

Most bobbles involve working into the same stitch and turning the rows on those stitches. Here the bobble is worked in stocking stitch on reverse stocking-stitch background. Create larger or smaller bobbles with fewer or more stitches or rows, or try contrasting the colour of the bobbles against the background.

Make Bobble (mb)

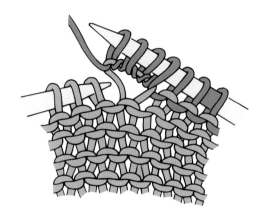

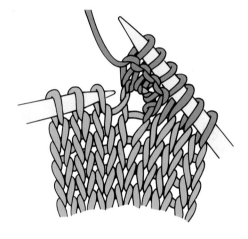

1 On a right side row work to the position of the bobble. Work [k1, p1] twice, all into next stitch. Slip the stitch off the left-hand needle so that the four new stitches are on the right-hand needle.

2 Turn the work so that the wrong side is facing and purl the four bobble stitches, then turn again and knit them. Turn and purl these 4 stitches again, thus making three rows in stocking stitch worked over the bobble stitches.

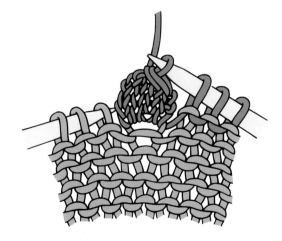

3 Turn the work so that the right side is facing. Slip the first two stitches onto the right-hand needle, knit the next two stitches together, then pass the two slipped stitches over the first stitch.

4 One stitch remains and you continue to work the remainder of the row as required. Any small gap in the fabric is hidden by the bobble when you continue knitting.

Aran Stitch Library

Now that you have an understanding of how to work cables and bobbles, you can practice the techniques on the wide variety of both cable and other Aran patterns given in this stitch library (see page 158 for abbreviations). Try working some swatches in different weights of yarn to test the results.

Simple Two-stitch Cables

Cable 2 Front (on left of photograph).
Panel of 2 sts on background of reverse st st.
1st row (right side) C2F.
2nd row P2.
Rep these 2 rows.
Cable 2 Back (on right of photograph).
Panel of 2 sts on background of reverse st st.
1st row (right side) C2B.
2nd row P2.
Rep these 2 rows.

Simple Four-stitch Cables

Cable 4 Front (on left of photograph).
Panel of 4 sts on background of reverse st st.
1st row (right side) K4.
2nd and 4th rows P4.
3rd row C4F.
Rep these 4 rows.
Cable 4 Back (on right of photograph).
Work as given for Cable 4 front but working C4B
in place of C4F.

Small Cable

Panel of 4 sts on background of reverse st st.
1st row (right side) C2B, C2F.
2nd row P4.
Rep these 2 rows.

Claw Pattern

Panel of 8 sts on background of reverse st st.
1st row (right side) K8.
2nd row P8.
3rd row C4B, C4F.
4th row P8.
Rep these 4 rows.

Little Pearl Cable

Panel of 4 sts on background of reverse st st.
1st row (right side) C2B, C2F.
2nd row P4.
3rd row C2F, C2B.
4th row P4.
Rep these 4 rows.

Up And Down Plait

Panel of 9 sts on background of reverse st st.
Up Plait (on left of photograph).
1st row (right side) K3, C6F.
2nd row P9.
3rd row C6B, k3.
4th row P9.
Rep these 4 rows.
Down Plait (on right of photograph).
Work as given for Up Plait but working C6B in
place of C6F and C6F in place of C6B.

Trinity Stitch

Multiple of 4 sts + 2 sts.
1st row (right side) Purl to end.
2nd row K1, *[K1, p1, k1] all in next st, p3tog; rep
from * to last st, k1.
3rd row Purl to end.
4th row K1, *p3tog, [k1, p1, k1] all in next st; rep
from * to last st, k1.
Rep these 4 rows.

Double Cable

Panel of 12 sts on background of reverse st st.
1st row (right side) K12.
2nd row P12.
3rd row C6B, C6F.
4th row P12.
5th and 6th rows As 1st and 2nd rows.
Rep these 6 rows.

Chevron Rib

Multiple of 12 sts + 3 sts.
1st row (right side) K3, *p2, Cr2R, k1, Cr2L, p2, k3; rep from * to end.
2nd row P3, *k2, p1, [k1, p1] twice, k2, p3; rep from * to end.
3rd row K3, *p1, Cr2R, p1, k1, p1, Cr2L, p1, k3; rep from * to end.
4th row P3, *k1, p1, [k2, p1] twice, k1, p3; rep from * to end.
5th row K3, *Cr2R, p2, k1, p2, Cr2L, k3; rep from * to end.
6th row P3, *k4, p1, k4, p3; rep from * to end
Rep these 6 rows.

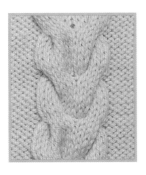

Chunky Double Cable

Panel of 16 sts on background of reverse st st.
1st row (right side) K16.
2nd row P16.
3rd row Slip next 4 sts onto cable needle and leave at back of work, k4, then k4 from cable needle, slip next 4 sts onto cable needle and leave at front of work, k4, then k4 from cable needle.
4th row P16.
5th to 8th rows Rep 1st and 2nd rows twice.
Rep these 8 rows.

Small Honeycomb Pattern

Multiple of 8 sts + 2 sts.
1st row K1, p2, [k4, p4] to last 7 sts, k4, p2, k1.
2nd row P1, k2, [p4, k4] to last 7 sts, p4, k2, p1.
3rd row K1, [Cr4B, Cr4F] rep to last st, k1.
4th and 6th rows P3, [k4, p4] to last 7 sts, k4, p3.
5th row K3, [p4, k4] to last 7 sts, p4, k3.
7th row K1, [Cr4F, Cr4B] rep to last st, k1.
8th row As 2nd row.
Rep these 8 rows.

Bobbles And Waves

Panel of 26 sts on background of reverse st st.
Special abbreviation: mb = make 3-st bobble thus: knit into front, back and front of next st, [turn and k3 sts] 3 times, turn, sl 1, k2tog, psso. Leave bobble on right side of work.
1st row (right side) P2, Cr3R, p5, C6B, p5, Cr3L, p2.
2nd row K2, p2, k6, p6, k6, p2, k2.
3rd row P1, Cr3R, p4, Cr5R, Cr5L, p4, Cr3L, p1.
4th row K1, p2, k5, p3, k4, p3, k5, p2, k1.
5th row Cr3R, p3, Cr5R, p4, Cr5L, p3, Cr3L.
6th row P2, k1, mb, k2, p3, k8, p3, k2, mb, k1, p2.
7th row Cr3L, p3, k3, p8, k3, p3, Cr3R.
8th row K1, p2, k3, p3, k8, p3, k3, p2, k1.
9th row P1, Cr3L, p2, Cr5L, p4, Cr5R, p2, Cr3R, p1.
10th row K2, p2, [k4, p3] twice, k4, p2, k2.

11th row P2,Cr3L, p3, Cr5L,Cr5R, p3,Cr3R, p2.
12th row K1, mb, k1, p2, k5, p6, k5, p2, k1, mb, k1.
Rep these 12 rows.

Oxo Cable

A panel of 8 sts on background of reverse st st.
1st row (right side) K8.
2nd row P8.
3rd row C4B, C4F.
4th row P8.
5th to 10th rows Rep these 4 rows once, then 1st and 2nd rows again.
11th row C4F, C4B.
12th row P8.
13th and 14th rows As 1st and 2nd rows.
15th and 16th rows As 11th and 12th rows.
Rep these 16 rows.

Cable Rib

Panel of 7 sts on background of reverse st st.
1st row (right side) K1, [p1, k1] 3 times.
2nd row P1 tbl, [k1, p1 tbl] 3 times.

3rd row Slip next 4 sts onto cable needle and leave at back of work, k1, p1, k1, then [p1, k1] twice from cable needle.
4th row As 2nd row.
5th and 6th rows As 1st and 2nd rows.
7th and 8th rows As 1st and 2nd rows.
9th and 10th rows As 1st and 2nd rows.
Rep these 10 rows.

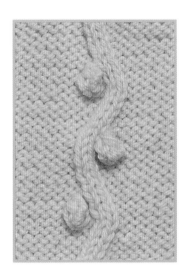

Wandering Cable With Bobbles

Panel of 6 sts on background of reverse st st.
Special abbreviation: mb = make 4 st bobble thus: [k1, p1] twice all in to next st, turn and p4, turn and sl 2, k2tog, pass 2 slipped sts over.
1st row (right side) P1, mb, p1, Cr3R.
2nd row K1, p2, k3.
3rd row P2, Cr3R, p1.
4th row K2, p2, k2.
5th row P1, Cr3R, p2.
6th row K3, p2, k1.
7th row Cr3R, p3.
8th row K4, p2.
9th row Cr3L, p1, mb, p1.
10th row K3, p2, k1.
11th row P1, Cr3L, p2.
12th row K2, p2, k2.
13th row P2, Cr3L, p1.
14th row K1, p2, k3.
15th row P3, Cr3L.
16th row P2, k4.
Rep these 16 rows.

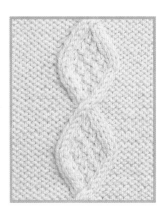

Framed Double Moss Stitch

Panel of 11 sts on background of reverse st st.
1st row (right side) P2, C3B, p1, C3F, p2.
2nd row K2, p3, k1, p3, k2.
3rd row P1, C3B, p1, k1, p1, C3F, p1.
4th row K1, p3, k1, p1, k1, p3, k1.
5th row C3B, p1, [k1, p1] twice, C3F.
6th row P3, k1, [p1, k1] twice, p3.
7th row K2, p1, [k1, p1] 3 times, k2.
8th row P2, k1, [p1, k1] 3 times, p2.
9th row Cr3L, p1, [k1, p1] twice, Cr3R.
10th row K1, p2, k1, [p1, k1] twice, p2, k1.
11th row P1, Cr3L, p1, k1, p1, Cr3R, p1.
12th row K2, p2, k1, p1, k1, p2, k2.
13th row P2, Cr3L, p1, Cr3R, p2.
14th row K3, p2, k1, p2, k3.
15th row P3, slip next 3 sts onto cable needle and leave at back of work, k2, k3 from cable needle, p3.
16th row K3, p5, k3.
Rep these 16 rows.

Bobble Fan

Panel of 11 sts on background of reverse st st.
Special abbreviation: mb = Make 4 st bobble thus: [k1, p1] twice all into next st, turn and p4, turn and k4, turn and p4, turn and sl 2, k2tog, pass 2 slipped stitches over.
1st row (right side) P11.
2nd row K11.
3rd row P5, mb, p5.
4th row K5, p1 tbl, k5.
5th row P2, mb, p2, k1 tbl, p2, mb, p2.
6th row K2, [p1 tbl, k2] 3 times.
7th row Mb, p1, Tw2L, p1, k1 tbl, p1, Tw2R, p1, mb.
8th row P1 tbl, k2, p1 tbl, [k1, p1 tbl] twice, k2, p1 tbl.
9th row Tw2L, p1, Tw2L, k1 tbl, Tw2R, p1, Tw2R.
10th row K1, Tw2RW, k1, [p1 tbl] 3 times, k1, Tw2LW, k1.
11th row P2, Tw2L, m1, sl 1, k2tog, psso, m1, Tw2R, p2.
12th row K3, Tw2RW, p1 tbl, Tw2LW, k3.
13th row P4, m1, sl 1, k2tog, psso, m1, p4.
14th row K5, p1 tbl, k5.
15th row P11.
16th row K11.
Rep these 16 rows.

Cupped Cable

Panel of 17 sts on background of reverse st st.
1st row (right side) K2, p4, k2, p1, k2, p4, k2.
2nd row K6, p2, k1, p2, k6.
3rd row P6, slip next 3 sts onto cable needle and leave at back of work, k2, then p1, k2 from cable needle, p6.
4th row As 2nd row.
5th row P5, Cr3R, k1, Cr3L, p5.
6th row K5, p2, k1, p1, k1, p2, k5.

7th row P4, Cr3R, k1, p1, k1, Cr3L, p4.
8th row K4, p2, k1, [p1, k1] twice, p2, k4.
9th row P3, Cr3R, k1, [p1, k1] twice, Cr3L, p3.
10th row K3, p2, k1, [p1, k1] 3 times, p2, k3.
11th row P2, Cr3R, k1, [p1, k1] 3 times, Cr3L, p2.
12th row K2, p2, k1, [p1, k1] 4 times, p2, k2.
13th row P1, Cr3R, k1, [p1, k1] 4 times, Cr3L, p1.
14th row K1, p2, k1, [p1, k1] 5 times, p2, k1.
15th row Cr3R, k1, [p1, k1] 5 times, Cr3L.
16th row P2, k1, [p1, k1] 6 times, p2.
Rep these 16 rows.

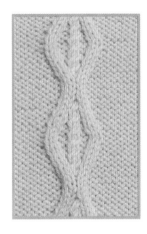

Big And Little Cable

Panel of 12 sts on background of reverse st st.
1st row (right side) P3, C3B, C3F, p3.
2nd row K3, p6, k3.
3rd row P2, Cr3R, C2B, Cr3L, p2.
4th row K2, p2, [k1, p2] twice, k2.
5th row P1, Cr3R, p1, C2B, p1, Cr3L, p1.
6th row K1, p2, [k2, p2] twice, k1.
7th row Cr3R, p2, C2B, p2, Cr3L.
8th row P2, [k3, p2] twice.
9th row Cr3L, p2, C2B, p2, Cr3R.
10th row As 6th row.
11th row P1, Cr3L, p1, C2B, p1, Cr3R, p1.
12th row As 4th row.
13th row P2, Cr3L, C2B, Cr3R, p2.
14th row K3, p6, k3.
15th row P3, Cr3L,Cr3R, p3.
16th row K4, p4, k4.
17th row P4, k4, p4.
18th row K4, p4, k4.
Rep these 18 rows.

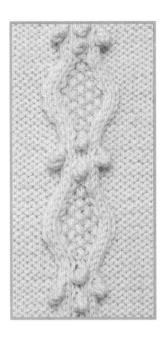

Hollow Oak

Panel of 11 sts on background of reverse st st.
Special abbreviation: mb = make 6 st bobble thus:
[k1, p1] 3 times all into next stitch, pass 2nd, then
3rd, 4th, 5th and 6th sts over first st.
1st row (right side) P3, k2, mb, k2, p3.
2nd row K3, p5, k3.
3rd row P3, mb, k3, mb, p3.
4th row K3, p5, k3.
5th and 6th rows As 1st and 2nd rows.
7th row P2, C3B, p1, C3F, p2.
8th row K2, p2, k1, p1, k1, p2, k2.
9th row P1, Cr3R, k1, p1, k1, Cr3L, p1.
10th row K1, p3, k1, p1, k1, p3, k1.
11th row C3B, p1, [k1, p1] twice, C3F.
12th row P2, k1, [p1, k1] 3 times, p2.
13th row K3, p1, [k1, p1] twice, k3.
14th row As 12th row.
15th row Cr3L, p1, [k1, p1] twice, Cr3R.
16th row As 10th row.
17th row P1, Cr3L, k1, p1, k1, Cr3R, p1.
18th row As 8th row.
19th row P2, Cr3L, p1, Cr3R, p2.
20th row K3, p5, k3.
Rep these 20 rows.

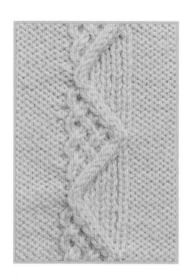

Cabled Hearts

Panel of 15 sts on background of reverse st st.
Note: due to the nature of the pattern the number of sts within the panel varies on some rows.
1st row (right side) P3, Cr2R, [k1, p1] twice, k1, Cr2L, p3.
2nd row K3, p2, [k1, p1] twice, k1, p2, k3.
3rd row P2, C2B, [p1, k1] 3 times, p1, C2F, p2.
4th row K2, [p1, k1] 5 times, p1, k2.
5th row P1, Cr2R, [k1, p1] twice, work into front, back and front of next st, [p1, k1] twice, Cr2L, p1. 17 sts.
6th row K1, p2, k1, p1, k1, p5, k1, p1, k1, p2, k1.
7th row C2B, [p1, k1] twice, p1, m1, k3, m1, [p1, k1] twice, p1, C2F. 19 sts.
8th row [P1, k1] 3 times, p7, [k1, p1] 3 times.
9th row K1 tbl, [k1, p1] 3 times, m1, k5, m1, [p1, k1] 3 times, k1 tbl. 21 sts.
10th row [P1, k1] 3 times, p9, [k1, p1] 3 times.
11th row K1 tbl, [k1, p1] 3 times, k2, sl 1, k2tog, psso, k2, [p1, k1] 3 times, k1 tbl. 19 sts.
12th row As 8th row.
13th row K1 tbl, [k1, p1] 3 times, k1, sl 1, k2tog, psso, k1, [p1, k1] 3 times, k1 tbl. 17 sts.
14th row [P1, k1] 3 times, p5, [k1, p1] 3 times.
15th row K1 tbl, [k1, p1] 3 times, yb, sl 1, k2tog, psso, [p1, k1] 3 times, k1 tbl. 15 sts.
16th row [P1, k1] 3 times, p3, [k1, p1] 3 times.
17th row Cr2L, p1, k1, p1, Cr2R, k1, Cr2L, p1, k1, p1, Cr2R.

18th row K1, p2, [k1, p3] twice, k1, p2, k1.
19th row P1, Cr2L, k1, C2B, p1, k1, p1, C2F, k1, Cr2R, p1.
20th row K4, [p1, k1] 3 times, p1, k4.
Rep these 20 rows.

Zigzag Lattice

Panel of 12 sts on background of reverse st st.
1st row (right side) [K1, p1] 4 times, Cr4R.
2nd row K1, p3, [k1, p1] 4 times.
3rd row [K1, p1] 3 times, Cr4R, Cr2L.
4th row P1, k2, p3, [k1, p1] 3 times.
5th row [K1, p1] twice, Cr4R, Cr2L, Cr2R.
6th row K1, C2BW, k2, p3, [k1, p1] twice.
7th row K1, p1, Cr4R, Cr2L, Cr2R, Cr2L.
8th row P1, k2, C2FW, k2, p3, k1, p1.
9th row Cr4R, [Cr2L, Cr2R] twice.
10th row K1, C2BW, k2, C2BW, k3, p2.
11th row Cr4L, [Cr2R, Cr2L] twice.
12th row As 8th row.
13th row K1, p1, Cr4L, Cr2R, Cr2L, Cr2R.
14th row As 6th row.
15th row [K1, p1] twice, Cr4L, Cr2R, Cr2L.
16th row As 4th row.
17th row [K1, p1] 3 times, Cr4L, Cr2R.
18th row As 2nd row.
19th row [K1, p1] 4 times, Cr4L.
20th row P2, [k1, p1] 5 times.
Rep these 20 rows.

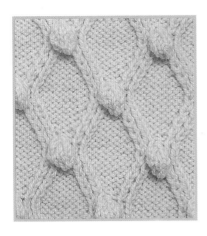

Trellis With Bobbles

Multiple of 16 sts + 5 sts.

Special abbreviation: mb = make 4-st bobble thus: [k1, p1] twice all into next st, [turn and p4, turn and k4] twice, turn and p4, turn and sl 2, k2tog, pass 2 slipped sts over.

1st row (right side) P6, [Cr2R] twice, p1, [Cr2L] twice, *p7, [Cr2R] twice, p1, [Cr2L] twice; rep from * to last 6 sts, p6.

2nd row K6, p1 tbl, k1, p1 tbl, k3, p1 tbl, k1, p1 tbl, *k7, p1 tbl, k1, p1 tbl, k3, p1 tbl, k1, p1 tbl; rep from * to last 6 sts, k6.

3rd row P5, *[Cr2R] twice, p3, [Cr2L] twice, p5; rep from * to end.

4th row K5, *p1 tbl, k1, p1 tbl, k5; rep from * to end.

5th row P4, *[Cr2R] twice, p5, [Cr2L] twice, p3; rep from * to last st, p1.

6th row K4, *p1 tbl, k1, p1 tbl, k7, p1 tbl, k1, p1 tbl, k3; rep from * to last st, k1.

7th row P3, *[Cr2R] twice, p7, [Cr2L] twice, p1; rep from * to last 2 sts, p2.

8th row K3, p1 tbl, k1, p1 tbl, k9, *[p1 tbl, k1] 3 times, p1 tbl, k9; rep from * to last 6 sts, p1 tbl, k1, p1 tbl, k3.

9th row P2, mb, *k1, p1, k1, p9, k1, p1, k1, mb; rep from * to last 2 sts, p2.

10th row As 8th row.

11th row P3, *[Cr2L] twice, p7, [Cr2R] twice, p1; rep from * to last 2 sts, p2.

12th row As 6th row.

13th row P4, *[Cr2L] twice, p5, [Cr2R] twice, p3; rep from * to last st, p1.

14th row As 4th row.

15th row P5, *[Cr2L] twice, p3, [Cr2R] twice, p5; rep from * to end.

16th row As 2nd row.

17th row P6, [Cr2L] twice, p1, [Cr2R] twice, *p7, [Cr2L] twice, p1, [Cr2R] twice; rep from * to last 6 sts, p6.

18th row K7, p1 tbl, [k1, p1 tbl] 3 times, *k9, p1 tbl, [k1, p1 tbl] 3 times; rep from * to last 7 sts, k7.

19th row P7, k1, p1, k1, mb, k1, p1, k1, *p9, k1, p1, k1, mb, k1, p1, k1; rep from * to last 7 sts, p7.

20th row As 18th row.

Rep these 20 rows.

Triple Twisted Cable

Panel of 26 sts on background of reverse st st.

1st row (right side) K6, [p4, k6] twice.

2nd row P6, [k4, p6] twice.

3rd row C6B, [p4, C6B] twice.

4th row As 2nd row.

5th to 8th rows As 1st to 4th rows.

9th row K3, Cr5L, p2, k6, p2, Cr5R, k3.

10th row [P3, k2] twice, p6, [k2, p3] twice.

11th row [Cr5L] twice, k6, [Cr5R] twice.

12th row K2, p3, k2, p12, k2, p3, k2.

13th row P2, Cr5L, [C6F] twice, Cr5R, p2.

14th row K4, p18, k4.

15th row P4, [C6B] 3 times, p4.

16th row K4, p18, k4.

17th row P2, Cr5R, [C6F] twice, Cr5L, p2.

18th row As 12th row.

19th row [Cr5R] twice, k6, [Cr5L] twice.

20th row As 10th row.

21st row K3, Cr5R, p2, k6, p2, Cr5L, k3.

22nd to 28th rows As 2nd to 8th rows.

Rep these 28 rows.

Project 5: Simple Cable Sweater

The 6-stitch cables worked across this design alternate between a back cross and a front cross, so working this project will help you achieve fluency with the cabling technique.

Materials

8(9:10) 50g balls of Rowan Designer DK Wool.
Pair each of 3¼mm (No 10/US 3) and 4mm (No 8/ US 6) knitting needles.
Cable needles.

Measurements

To fit age	2-3	4-5	6-7	years
Actual chest	68	84	100	cm
measurement	27	33	39½	in
Length	34	43	49	cm
	13½	17	19¼	in
Sleeve seam	25	28	32	cm
	10	11	12½	in

Tension

30 sts and 32 rows to 10cm/4in square over cable pattern on 4mm (No 8/US 6) needles.

Abbreviations

C6B = sl next 3 sts onto cable needle and leave at back of work, k3, then k3 from cable needle;
C6F = sl next 3 sts onto cable needle and leave at front of work, k3, then k3 from cable needle.
Also see page 158.

Back

With 3¼mm (No 10/US 3) needles cast on 102 (126:150) sts.
1st rib row (right side) P2, [k2, p2] to end.
2nd rib row K2, [p2, k2] to end.
Rep last 2 rows 4 times more.
Change to 4mm (No 8/US 6) needles.
1st row P2, k2, p2, [k6, p2, k2, p2] to end.
2nd row K2, p2, k2, [p6, k2, p2, k2] to end.
3rd and 4th rows As 1st and 2nd rows.
5th row P2, k2, p2, [C6F, p2, k2, p2, C6B, p2, k2, p2] to end.
6th row As 2nd row.
7th and 8th rows As 1st and 2nd rows.
These 8 rows form cable patt. Cont in cable patt until work measures 32(41:47)cm/12¾(16¼:18½)in from beg,
ending with a wrong side row.
Shape Neck
Next row Patt 35(45:55), turn.
Work on this set of sts only for right back neck. Keeping patt correct, dec one st at neck edge on next 5 rows. 30(40:50) sts.
Shape Shoulder
Cast off 10(13:16) sts at beg of next row and foll alt row. Work 1 row. Cast off rem 10(14:18) sts.
With right side facing, sl centre 32(36:40) sts onto a holder, rejoin yarn to rem sts for left back neck and patt to end. Dec one st at neck edge on next 5 rows. 30(40:50) sts. Patt 1 row.
Shape Shoulder
Cast off 10(13:16) sts at beg of next row and foll alt row. Work 1 row. Cast off rem 10(14:18) sts.

Front

Work as given for Back until work measures 29(38:44)cm/11½(15:17¼)in from beg, ending with a wrong side row.
Shape Neck
Next row Patt 41(51:61), turn.
Work on this set of sts only for left front neck. Dec one st at neck edge on every row until 30(40:50) sts rem. Cont straight until front matches back to shoulder shaping, ending at side edge.
Shape Shoulder
Cast off 10(13:16) sts at beg of next row and foll alt row. Work 1 row. Cast off rem 10(14:18) sts.
With right side facing, sl centre 20(24:28) sts onto a holder, rejoin yarn to rem sts for right side neck, patt to end. Complete as given for left front neck.

Sleeves

With 3¼mm (No 10/US 3) needles cast on 50(50:58) sts.
1st rib row (right side) K2, [p2, k2] to end.
2nd rib row P2, [k2, p2] to end.
Rep these 2 rows 4 times more.
Change to 4mm (No 8/US 6) needles.
1st row (right side) [K2, p2] 1(1:2) times, [k6, p2, k2, p2] 3 times, k6, [p2, k2] 1(1:2) times.
2nd row [P2, k2] 1(1:2) times, [p6, k2, p2, k2] 3 times, p6, [k2, p2] 1(1:2) times.

3rd and 4th rows As 1st and 2nd rows.
5th row [K2, p2] 1(1:2) times, C6F, p2, k2, p2, C6B, p2, k2, p2, C6F, p2, k2, p2, C6B, [p2, k2] 1(1:2) times.
6th row As 2nd row.
7th and 8th rows As 1st and 2nd rows.
These 8 rows form cable patt. Cont in cable patt, inc one st at each end of 1st row and 4(8:4) foll 2nd rows, then on every foll 4th row until there are 80(88:96) sts, working inc sts into patt. Cont straight until work measures 25(28:32)cm/10(11:12½)in from beg, ending with a wrong side row. Cast off in patt.

Collar

Join right shoulder seam.
With 3¼mm (No 10/US 3) needles and right side facing, k up 17 sts down left side of front neck, k centre front sts, k up 16 sts up right side of front neck, 6 sts down right side of back neck, k centre back sts, k up 7 sts up left side of back neck. 98(106:114) sts.
1st rib row K2(0:2), [p2, k2] to last 0(2:0) sts, p0(2:0).
2nd rib row P2(0:2), [k2, p2] to last 0(2:0) sts, k0(2:0).
Rep these 2 rows 4(5:6) times more.
Change to 4mm (No 8/US 6) needles,
Rib a further 12(14:16) rows. Cast off loosely in rib.

To Make Up (see also Finishing Workshop)

Join left shoulder and collar seam, reversing seam half way up on collar. Mark depth of armholes approximately 14(15:16)cm/5½(6:6½)in down from shoulders at side edges of back and front. Sew cast off edge of sleeves between markers. Join side and sleeve seams.

Project 6: Aran Throw

The throw uses a large, slightly more complex cable combined with a simple 4-stitch cable and garter stitch. This design gives you the opportunity to work different stitch patterns across the row, which is what you will be doing when you tackle Aran garments in the future.

Materials

20 50g balls of Rowan DK Handknit Cotton.
Pair of long 4mm (No 8/US 6) knitting needles.
Cable needle.

Measurements

Approximately 84cm x 122cm/33in x 48in.

Tension

20 sts and 28 rows to 10cm/4in square over st st on 4mm (No 8/US 6) needles.

Abbreviations

C4B = sl next 2 sts onto cable needle and leave at back of work, k2, then k2 from cable needle.
Also see page 158.

To Make

With 4mm (No 8/US 6) needles cast on 175 sts.
K 13 rows.
Inc row: K9, *k twice in next st, k8, [k twice in next st, k3] twice, k twice in next st, k8; rep from * 5 times more, k twice in next st, k9. 200 sts.
Foundation row K8, p4, [k7, p2, k2, p4, k2, p2, k7, p4] 6 times, k8.
Work in patt as follows:
1st row (right side) K7, p1, k4, [p1, k4, p2, k2, p2, k4, p2, k2, p2, k4, p1, k4] 6 times, p1, k7.
2nd row K8, p4, [k7, p2, k2, p4, k2, p2, k7, p4] 6 times, k8.
3rd row K7, p1, C4B, [p1, k4, p2, k2, p2, k4, p2, k2, p2, k4, p1, C4B] 6 times, p1, k7.
4th row As 2nd row.
5th to 8th rows As 1st to 4th rows.
9th row K7, p1, k4, [p1, k4, p2, sl next 4 sts onto cable needle and leave at back of work, k2, then p2, k2 from cable needle, sl next 2 sts onto cable needle and leave at front of work, k2, p2, then k2 from cable needle, p2, k4, p1, k4] 6 times, p1, k7.

10th to 12th rows As 2nd to 4th rows.
13th to 15th rows As 1st to 3rd rows.
16th row K8, p4, [k26, p4] 6 times, k8.
17th row K7, p1, k4, [p1, k24, p1, k4] 6 times, p1, k7.
18th row As 16th row.
19th row K7, p1, C4B, [p1, k24, p1, C4B] 6 times, p1, k7.
20th row As 16th row.
These 20 rows form patt. Rep them 17 times more, then work 1st to 14th rows again.
Dec row K9, *k2tog, k8, [k2tog, k3] twice, k2tog, k8; rep from * 5 times more, k2tog, k9. 175 sts.
K 12 rows. Cast off knitwise.

Project 7: Child's Aran Coat

This classic design has a neat garter-stitch collar and hem with a bobble detail that echoes the cable pattern. The technique of working into the back of the cable stitches creates a more defined pattern.

Materials

8(9) 100g hanks of Rowan Magpie Aran.
Pair each of 4mm (No 8/US 6) and 5mm (No 6/US 8) knitting needles.
Cable needle.
9 buttons.

Measurements

To fit age		4-6	7-10	years
Actual chest measurement		96	108	cm
		38	42½	in
Length		52	58	cm
		20½	22¾	in
Sleeve seam		29	38	cm
		11½	15	in

Tensions

17 sts and 25 rows to 10cm/4in square over st st on 5mm (No 6/US 8) needles.
15 sts of panel A pattern measures 6cm/2½in and 21 sts of panel B pattern measures 8.5cm/3¼in on 5mm (No 6/US 8) needles.

Abbreviations

C3B = sl next st onto cable needle and leave at back of work, k2, then k1tbl from cable needle;
C3F = sl next 2 sts onto cable needle and leave at front of work, k1tbl, then k2 from cable needle;
C5 = sl next 3 sts onto cable needle and leave at back of work, k2, then p1, k2 from cable needle;
Cr3L = sl next 2 sts onto cable needle and leave at front of work, p1, then k2 from cable needle;
Cr3R = sl next st onto cable needle and leave at back of work, k2, then p1 from cable needle;
Cr4L = sl next 3 sts onto cable needle and leave at front of work, k1, then k1 tbl, p1, k1 tbl from cable needle;
Cr4R = sl next st onto cable needle and leave at back of work, k1 tbl, p1, k1 tbl, then k1 from cable needle;
mb = knit into front, back, front, back and front of next st, turn, p5, turn, k3, k2tog, then pass 2nd, 3rd and 4th st over the 1st st.
Also see page 158.

Panel A

Worked over 15 sts.
1st row (right side) P4, C3B, p1, C3F, p4.
2nd row K4, p3, k1, p3, k4.
3rd row P3, Cr3R, k1 tbl, p1, k1 tbl, Cr3L, p3.
4th row K3, p2, k1, [p1, k1] twice, p2, k3.
5th row P2, C3B, p1, [k1t tbl, p1] twice, C3F, p2.
6th row K2, p3, k1, [p1, k1] twice, p3, k2.
7th row P1, Cr3R, k1 tbl, [p1, k1 tbl] 3 times, Cr3L, p1.
8th row K1, p2, k1, [p1, k1] 4 times, p2, k1.
9th row P1, Cr3L, k1 tbl, [p1, k1 tbl] 3 times, Cr3R, p1.
10th row As 6th row.
11th row P2, Cr3L, p1, [k1 tbl, p1] twice, Cr3R, p2.
12th row As 4th row.
13th row P3, Cr3L, k1 tbl, p1, k1 tbl, Cr3R, p3.
14th row As 2nd row.
15th row P4, Cr3L, p1, Cr3R, p4.
16th row K5, p2, k1, p2, k5.
17th row P5, C5, p5.
18th row As 16th row.
19th row P4, Cr3R, p1, Cr3L, p4.
20th row K4, p2, k3, p2, k4.
21st row P3, Cr3R, p3, Cr3L, p3.
22nd row K3, p2, k5, p2, k3.
23rd row P3, Cr3L, p3, Cr3R, p3.
24th row As 20th row.
25th to 28th rows Work 15th to 18th rows.
These 28 rows form patt.

Panel B

Worked over 21 sts.
1st row (right side) P6, Cr4R, k1tbl, Cr4L, p6.
2nd row K6, p1, [k1, p1] 4 times, k6.
3rd row P5, Cr4R, k1, k1 tbl, k1, Cr4L, p5.
4th row K5, p1, k1, p1, [k2, p1] twice, k1, p1, k5.
5th row P4, Cr4R, k2, k1 tbl, k2, Cr4L, p4.
6th row K4, p1, k1, p2, k2, p1, k2, p2, k1, p1, k4.
7th row P3, Cr4R, k1 tbl, [k2, k1 tbl] twice, Cr4L, p3.
8th row K3, p1, [k1, p1] twice, [k2, p1] twice, [k1, p1] twice, k3.
9th row P2, Cr4R, k1, k1 tbl, [k2, k1 tbl] twice, k1, Cr4L, p2.
10th row K2, p1, k1, p1, [k2, p1] 4 times, k1, p1, k2.
11th row P1, Cr4R, k2, [k1 tbl, k2] 3 times, Cr4L, p1.

12th row [K1, p1] twice, k3, [p1, k2] twice, p1, k3, [p1, k1] twice.

13th row [P1, k1t tbl] twice, k3, mb, [k2, mb] twice, k3, [k1 tbl, p1] twice.

14th row [K1, p1] twice, k3, p1 tbl, [k2, p1 tbl] twice, k3, [p1, k1] twice.

15th row [P1, k1 tbl] twice, p3, k1 tbl, p1, k3 tbl, p1, k1 tbl, p3, [k1 tbl, p1] twice.

16th row K7, p1, k1, p3, k1, p1, k7.

These 16 rows form patt.

Panel C

Worked over 5 sts.

1st to 4th rows P5.

5th row (right side) P2, mb, p2.

6th to 8th rows P5.

These 8 rows form patt.

Back

With 4mm (No 8/US 6) needles cast on 103(113) sts.
P 2 rows.

Next row P7(1), [mb, p10] 8(10) times, mb, p7(1).
P 2 rows.

Inc row P7(12), [p twice in next st, p7] 11 times, p twice in next st, p7(12). 115(125) sts.

Change to 5mm (No 6/US 8) needles.

1st row (right side) P0(5), ★k1 tbl, work 1st row of panel A, k1 tbl, work 1st row of panel B, k1 tbl, work 1st row of panel A, k1 tbl★; work 1st row of panel C, rep from ★ to ★, p0(5).

2nd row P0(5), ★p1 tbl, work 2nd row of panel A, p1 tbl, work 2nd row of panel B, p1 tbl, work 2nd row of panel A, p1 tbl★; work 2nd row of panel C, rep from ★ to ★, p0(5).

These 2 rows set position of panels. Cont in patt as set until back measures 52(58)cm/20½(22¾)in from beg, ending with a wrong side row.

Shape Shoulders

Cast off 18(20) sts at beg of next 2 rows and 19(20) sts at beg of foll 2 rows. Cast off rem 41(45) sts.

Left Front

With 4mm (No 8/US 6) needles cast on 54(59) sts.
P 2 rows.

Next row P4(9), [mb, p10] 4 times, mb, p5.
P 2 rows.

Inc row [P7, p twice in next st] 6 times, p6(11). 60(65) sts.

Change to 5mm (No 6/US 8) needles.

1st row (right side) P0(5), k1 tbl, work 1st row of panel A, k1 tbl, work 1st row of panel B, k1 tbl, work 1st row of panel A, k1 tbl, p5.

2nd row P5, p1 tbl, work 2nd row of panel A, p1 tbl,

work 2nd row of panel B, p1 tbl, work 2nd row of panel A, p1 tbl, p0(5).

These 2 rows set position of panels with p5 sts for front band. Cont in patt as set until front measures 45(51)cm/17¾(20)in from beg, ending at side edge.

Shape Neck

Next row Patt to last 6 sts, turn; leave these 6 sts on a safety pin.

Keeping patt correct, cast off 3(4) sts at beg of next row and foll alt row. Dec one st at neck edge on every row until 37(40) sts rem. Cont straight until front matches back to shoulder shaping, ending at side edge.

Shape Shoulder

Cast off 18(20) sts at beg of next row. Work 1 row. Cast off rem 19(20) sts.

Mark front band to indicate position of 7 buttons: first one to be made on 3rd row of welt, last one 1cm/¼in below neck shaping and rem 5 evenly spaced between.

Right Front

With 4mm (No 8/US 6) needles cast on 54(59) sts.
P 2 row.

Buttonhole row P2, yrn, p2 tog, p1, [mb, p10] 4 times, mb, p4(9).
P 2 rows.

Inc row P6(11), [p twice in next st, p7] 6 times. 60(65) sts.

Change to 5mm (No 6/US 8) needles.

1st row (right side) P5, k1 tbl, work 1st row of panel A, k1 tbl, work 1st row of panel B, k1 tbl, work 1st row of panel A, k1 tbl, p0(5).

2nd row P0(5), p1 tbl, work 2nd row of panel A, p1 tbl, work 2nd row of panel B, p1 tbl, work 2nd row of panel A, p1 tbl, p5.

These 2 rows set position of panels with p5 sts for front band.

Complete as given for left front making buttonholes to match markers as before.

Sleeves

With 4mm (No 8/US 6) needles cast on 33(37) sts.
P 2 rows.

Next row P4(6), [mb, p5] 4 times, mb, p4(6).
P 2 rows.

Inc row P1(2), [m1, p1, m1, p2] to last 2 sts, [m1, p1] twice. 55(61) sts.

Change to 5mm (No 6/US 8) needles.

1st row (right side) P0(3), k1 tbl, work 1st row of panel A, k1 tbl, work 1st row of panel B, k1 tbl, work 1st row of panel A, k1 tbl, p0(3).

2nd row P0(3), p1 tbl, work 2nd row of panel A, p1 tbl, work 2nd row of panel B, p1 tbl, work 2nd row of panel A, p1 tbl, p0(3).

These 2 rows set position of panels. Cont in patt as set,

inc one st at each end of 3rd row and every foll 5th(6th) row until there are 75(85) sts, purling inc sts on every row. Cont straight until sleeve measures 29(38)cm/11½(15)in from beg, ending with a wrong side row. Cast off.

Collar

Join shoulder seams.
With right side facing and using 4mm (No 8/US 6) needles, slip the 6 sts from right front safety pin onto needle, k up 20(21) sts up right front neck, 31(35) sts across back neck, 20(21) sts down left front neck, then p6 sts from safety pin. 83(89) sts.
P 1 row.
Next 2 rows P to last 23 sts, turn.
Next 2 rows P to last 19 sts, turn.
Next 2 rows P to last 15 sts, turn.
Next 2 rows P to last 11 sts, turn.
Next 2 rows P to last 7 sts, turn.
Next row P to end.

Cast off purlwise 3 sts at beg of next 2 rows. 77(83) sts.
P 4 rows.
Change to 5mm (No 6/US 8) needles.
Next row P2, mb, p to last 3 sts, mb, p2.
P 5 rows. Rep last 6 rows once more.
Next row P2, mb, [p5, mb] to last 2 sts, p2.
P 3 rows. Cast off loosely purlwise.

Belt

With 4mm (No 8/US 6) needles cast on 61 sts.
K 9 rows. Cast off.

To Make Up (see also Finishing Workshop)

Sew on sleeves, placing centre of sleeves to shoulder seams. Join side and sleeve seams. Sew on buttons. Place belt on back in required position and secure ends with buttons.

Above I like to use cable patterns together that have a common theme: here twisted stitches are used in both the cables and the dividing stitch. As this coat is worked in an Aran yarn, you only need a few rows to create a large bobble.

CHAPTER FOUR

Colour Workshop

THERE HAS NEVER BEEN a greater opportunity to create wonderful knits with colour. Spinners have extended their shade ranges to include not only pastels and primaries but also palettes with spicy ochres and terracottas, faded denims and citrus brights. This enables the knitter not only to produce both strong, dramatic effects and also subtle colour shadings.

Over the years I have met many experienced knitters who work intricately textured knits but lack confidence in working in colour and have avoided it. This is a shame as the techniques required are simple to learn and easy to put into practice.

Colour work is divided into two techniques, Fair Isle and intarsia. Fair Isle is used when colours run across the row, with the colour not in use being stranded at the back or woven in. Intarsia is where separate balls or lengths of yarn are used in individual areas of colour.

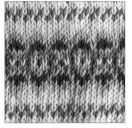

Three of the projects in this workshop demonstrate both of these techniques: the baby blanket is a patchwork of texture and colour using the intarsia technique, the cardigan is worked in Fair Isle and the child's sweater combines both techniques. There is also a simple striped hat which is knitted in the round on double pointed needles.

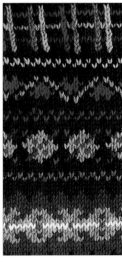

Joining In New Yarn

*When starting a new ball of yarn or working stripes in colour knitting, knowing where and how to join
in new yarn helps prevent unsightly knitting and untidy finishing and avoids weak spots.*

Whenever possible join in new yarn at the start of a
row. To estimate whether you have sufficient yarn to
complete a row of stocking stitch or plain fabric, lay
the work flat and see if the yarn reaches four times
across the width – that is the length you need to
finish a stocking stitch row.

For a heavily textured or patterned garment, if in
doubt join in the new ball at the start of the row to
avoid running out of yarn within a row and having
to unpick stitches worked. If you are sure you have
enough for one row, but unsure if there is enough
for two, tie a knot halfway along the remaining yarn.
Work one row; if you have not reached the knot you
know that there is enough to work another row.

To make a perfect join at the edge of your work,
simply drop the old yarn and start working the next
row with the new yarn. After a few stitches, tie the

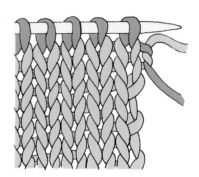

ends in a loose knot – they can be darned into the
seam later. If it is impossible to avoid joining in the
middle of a row, just drop the old yarn, leaving
sufficient length to sew in, pick up the new yarn,
leaving a sufficient length, and continue knitting.
Darn in the loose ends after a few rows.

Securing Ends

*Securing loose ends on a completed garment, particularly when it is a Fair Isle design, often
seems to take as long as the actual knitting did. However, do not rush or ignore this part of the
project as the fabric will eventually show up holes and ends, and other knitters can never resist
turning a garment inside out to check how neatly the back has been finished.*

An end or yarn simply woven around the stitches
can sometimes work itself loose once the garment is
worn and washed. One way to secure the end
properly is to weave the yarn loosely around a few
stitches, then double back on the woven-in end.
Make sure that the yarn is not pulled tightly as it
will distort the knitting. Stretch the fabric before
cutting the yarn to loosen the woven-in end. Make
sure also that the woven-in end is not visible from
the right side.

Never tie knots in the yarn as these will almost
invariably come undone or work their way through

to the right side. Any knots found in the yarn while
working should also be undone.

When using the intarsia method of colour
knitting (see page 72) leave a long end of yarn at the
beginning and end of each area of colour – as they
are within the work it is important to secure them
carefully. Draw the end up firmly before securing,
otherwise the stitch will appear loose on the right
side. The ends should be run along the line of
colour change on the wrong side as this will be less
visible on the right side.

Working From A Chart

Knitting patterns, particularly those dealing with colour work, are now often presented as charts rather than written out row by row. I like to work from charts as I find that it is so easy to check that the knitting matches the charted symbols.

A Fair Isle pattern given in chart form gives a visual impression of how the design will look when knitted. A single pattern repeat of the complete design (which is worked across the width and depth of the fabric) is shown as a chart on a squared grid. The colours in the pattern are either represented by symbols that are identified in a key, or the squares are shaded in a relevant colour. In this book symbols are used throughout.

Reading a chart is easier if you visualise it as a piece of knitting working from the lower edge to the top. Horizontally across the grid each square represents a stitch and vertically up the grid each square represents a row of knitting.

Generally the following rules apply.

Rows: for stocking stitch, work across a line of squares from right to left for the knit rows, then follow the line immediately above from left to right for the purl rows. To make following a chart easier, use a row counter (see page 11) or place a ruler under the row being worked and move the ruler up as each row is completed.

Stitches: usually only one repeat of the pattern is given in the chart and this has to be repeated across the width of the material. This section is usually contained within bold vertical lines with an indication that it is to be repeated across the row. There may be extra stitches at either end which are edge stitches worked at the beginning and end of rows to 'balance' the pattern out and to take up those remaining stitches that cannot be worked as a whole pattern repeat.

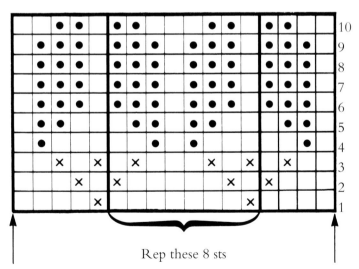

Rep these 8 sts

Edge stitches   Edge stitches

KEY

☒ Contrast colour A

☐ Main colour (M)

⦿ Contrast colour B

Fair Isle Knitting

Stranding is used when the yarn not in use is left at the back of the work until needed. The loops formed by stranding are called 'floats' and it is important to ensure that they are not pulled too tightly when working the next stitch as this will pull in your knitting. If the gap between the colours is more than 4 stitches the weaving in method is preferable as this prevents too long floats that stop the fabric having the right amount of elasticity. Many colour patterns will use both techniques and you will choose the one that is the most appropriate to a particular part of the design.

Weaving

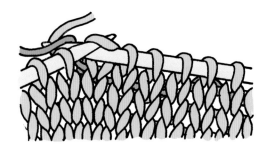

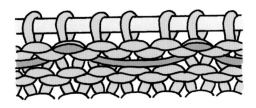

In weaving in, or knitting in, the floats are caught in by the working yarn on every alternate stitch, or preferably on every third or fourth stitch. (Weaving in on every alternate stitch can distort the stitches and alter the tension.)
Insert the right-hand needle into the stitch. Lay the

contrast yarn over the point of the right-hand needle then knit the stitch in the usual way, taking care not to knit in the contrast yarn. When you knit the next stitch, the contrast yarn will have been caught in. Use the same method to catch in the yarn on the purl rows.

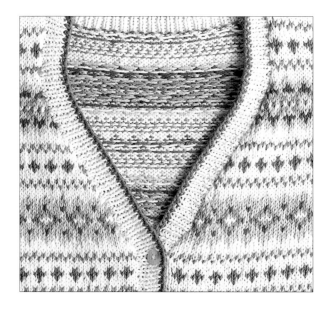

Left This detail of Project 10: Fair Isle Cardigan (see page 90) clearly shows how neat the back of woven and stranded fabric can be.

Stranding

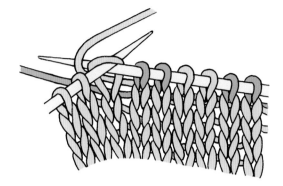

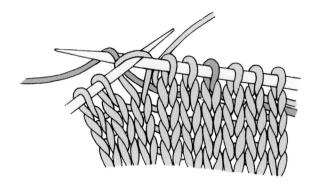

1 On a knit row, hold the first colour in your right hand and the second colour in your left hand. Knit the required number of stitches as usual with the first colour, carrying the second colour loosely across the wrong side of the work.

2 To knit a stitch in the second colour, insert the right-hand needle into the next stitch then draw a loop through from the yarn held in the left hand, carrying the yarn in the right hand loosely across the wrong side until required.

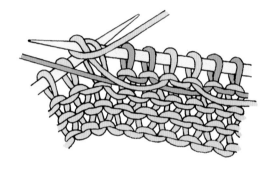

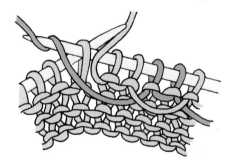

3 On a purl row, hold the yarns as for the knit rows. Purl the required number of stitches as usual with the first colour, carrying the second colour loosely across these stitches on the wrong side of the work.

4 To purl a stitch in the second colour, insert the right-hand needle into the next stitch then draw a loop through from the yarn held in the left hand, carrying the yarn in the right hand loosely across the wrong side until next required.

TIPS: FANCY YARNS

Colour knitting offers a wonderful opportunity to incorporate fancy yarns into garments. Gold and silver lurex yarns tend to look garish on their own, but can add subtle sparkle and a touch of glamour to knitwear when used in small quantities. Try working lurex into a Fair Isle pattern to give new touch to a traditional design. It can also be effective as a trim or edging for

collars and cuffs (see Decorative Details Stitch Library, pages 136-139 for edging patterns) or when used to embroider on to knitting (see pages 128-129). Mohair and angora yarns can work well on collars and cuffs, or try using them to make fake fur (see pages 130-131). Do experiment with combining different types of yarn; the results can be wonderful.

Intarsia Knitting

Intarsia is the name given to colour knitting where the pattern is worked in large blocks of colour at a time, requiring separate ball of yarn for each area of colour as the yarn must not be stranded at the back.

Diagonal Colour Change With A Slant To The Left

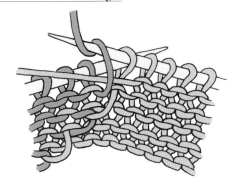

This diagram shows a colour change on the wrong side of the work.

Use separate balls of yarn for each block of colour. On a right side row, with the yarns at the back of the work, the crossing of colours at joins happens automatically because of the encroaching nature of the pattern. On a wrong side row, with the yarns at the front of the work, take the first colour over the second colour, drop it then pick up the second colour underneath the first colour thus crossing the two colours together.

Diagonal Colour Change With A Slant To The Right

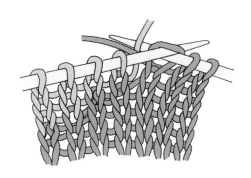

This diagram shows a colour change on the right side of the work.

Use separate balls of yarn for each block of colour. On a right side row, with the yarns at the back of the work, take the first colour over the second colour, drop it then pick up the second colour underneath the first colour thus crossing the two colours over. On a wrong side row, with the yarns at the front of the work, the crossing of the two colours at the joins happens automatically because of the encroaching nature of the pattern.

Vertical Colour Change

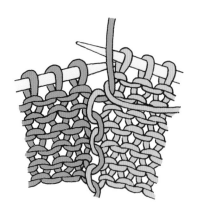

This diagram shows a colour change on the wrong side of the work.

Use separate balls of yarn for each block of colour. Work in the first colour to the colour change, then drop the first colour, pick up the second colour underneath the first colour, crossing the two colours over before working the next stitch in the second colour. The first stitch after a colour change is worked firmly to avoid a gap forming between colours. This technique ensures that the yarns are crossed on every row and gives a neat vertical line between colours on the right side, and a vertical line of loops in each colour on the wrong side.

Working In The Round

This form of knitting produces a seamless fabric which, without shaping, 'grows' into a tube.

Using A Circular Needle

To start work cast on to one of the points of the needle the number of stitches required, then spread them evenly along the complete length of the needle. At this stage it is vital to check that the cast-on edge is not twisted before you join the stitches into a ring. If it is twisted you will end up with a permanently twisted piece of material.

The first stitch that you work in the first round is the beginning of the round. To keep track of the beginning and end of the rounds, make a slip knot in a short length of contrasting coloured yarn and place it on the needle as a marker (this is known as a slip marker) at the start of the first round. Slip it from the point of one needle to the other at the beginning of every round.

Using A Set Of Four Needles

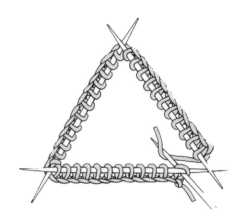

Divide the total number of stitches by three and cast that number on to each of three of the needles (the fourth one is the working needle). Form the needles into a triangle by drawing up the last cast-on stitch to meet the first one – taking care that the cast-on edge is not twisted. Knit the stitches from the first needle onto the fourth needle, and as each needle becomes free it becomes the working needle for the next group of stitches.

Pull the yarn up firmly at the changeover points to avoid a ladder forming or vary the changeover points by working two stitches from the next needle on each round. Keep track of the beginning of a round with a slip marker (see *Using A Circular Needle*).

TIPS: USING BOBBINS

Where two or more colours are used in a row, or when the same colour is used in a number of different places, it can be difficult to avoid tangling the yarns. Bobbins keep the yarns separate and allow them to hang at the back of the work until they are needed. Bobbins are ideal for motif knitting where only a short length of each colour is needed for different areas. Use a separate bobbin for each strand of yarn, wind on enough for each area of colour, and unwind short lengths as necessary when you are working.

Colour Stitch Library

The following stitch library consists of both single motifs and patterns that repeat across the row. Some variations on patterns are given as charts only. A multitude of different effects can be obtained from one pattern by working it in different shades and weights of yarn. Experiment by working a Fair Isle pattern in pastels in a fine yarn and then reworking it in brights on a dark background in a thicker yarn.

Stars

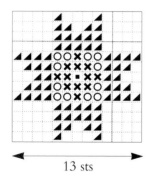

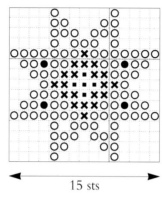

15 sts

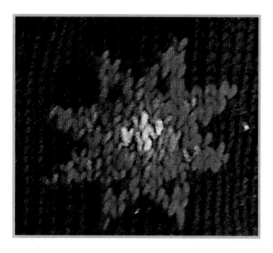

13 sts

Repeating Stars

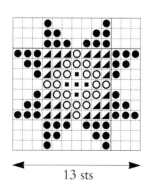

13 sts

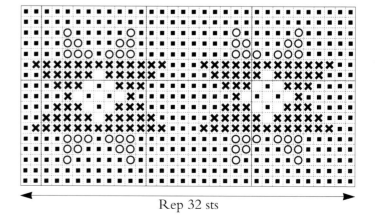

Rep 32 sts

Flowers

Pansy

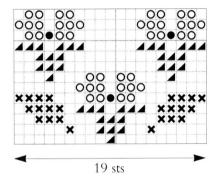

19 sts

Roses

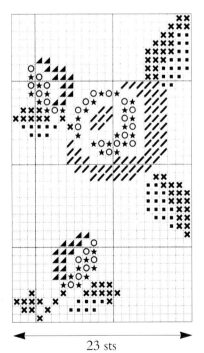

23 sts

Tulips And Heart

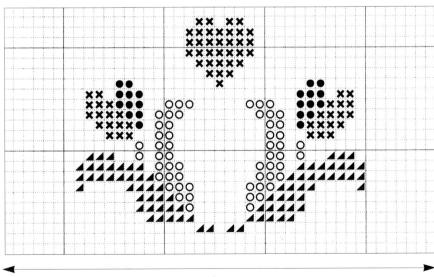

43 sts

Birds

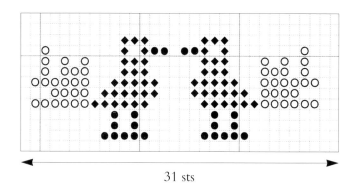

31 sts

Hearts

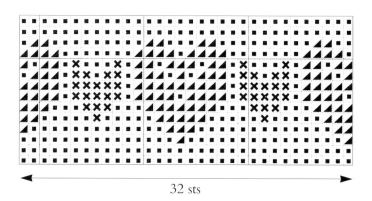

32 sts

Seaside

Fish

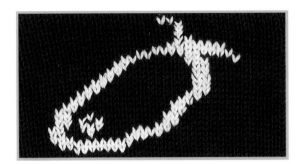

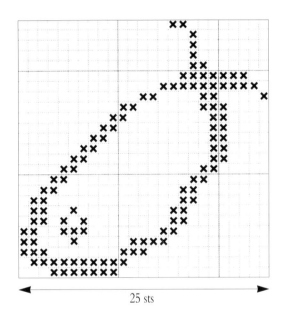

25 sts

Starfish

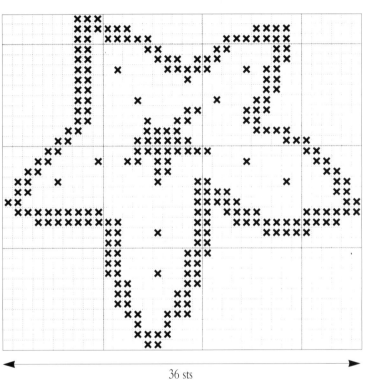

36 sts

Boat

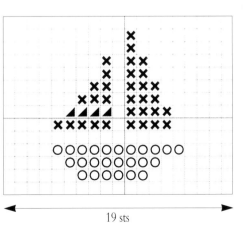

19 sts

Shell

Flags

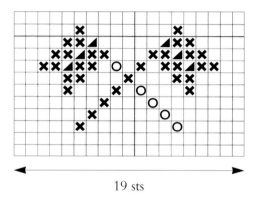

19 sts

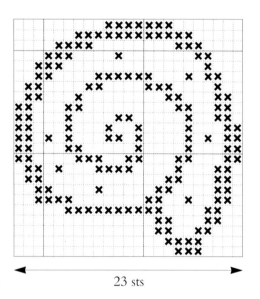

23 sts

Anchor

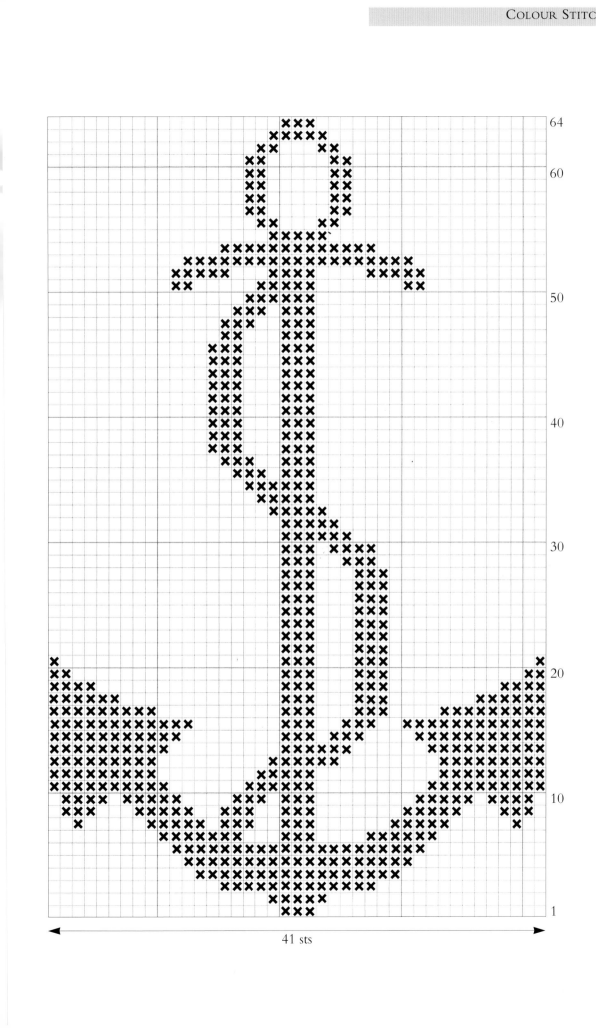

64

60

50

40

30

20

10

1

41 sts

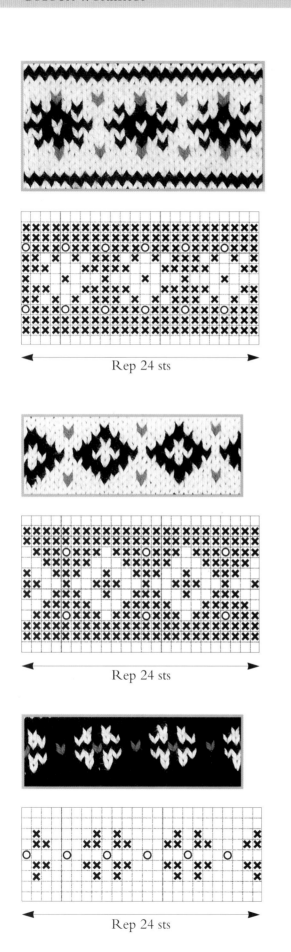

Rep 24 sts

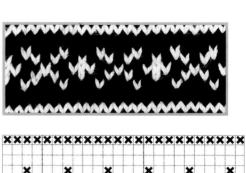

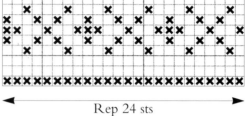

Rep 24 sts

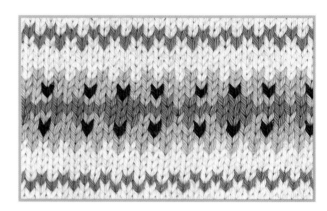

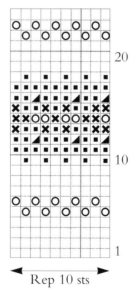

20

10

1

Rep 10 sts

Extended Fair Isles

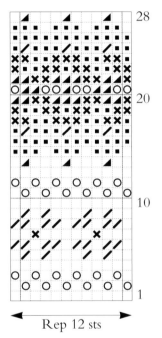

Rep 12 sts

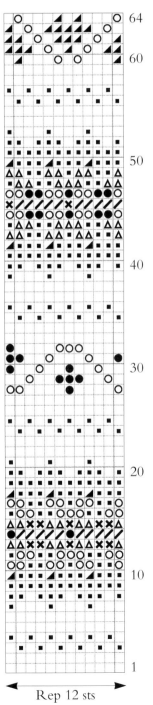

Rep 12 sts

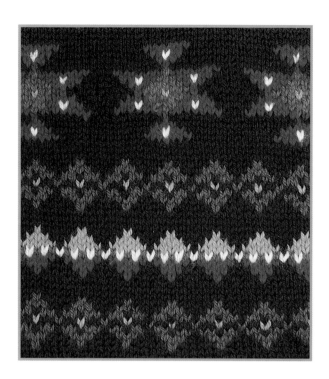

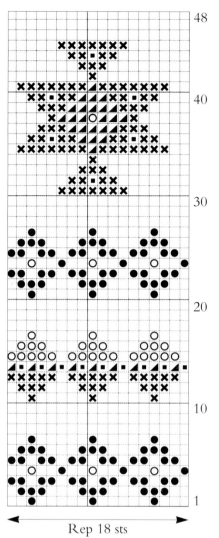

Rep 18 sts

TIPS: TRANSLATING PATTERNS

If you want to introduce a new motif into a design, a good way to start is by looking at cross-stitch or embroidery books to see if there are any patterns you can adapt to knitting. Although one square will represent one stitch, remember that in knitting a stitch is wider than a row is deep, so your designs will broaden out when knitted up. To compensate for this you can

add some rows. (If you were trying to achieve a circle in knitting you would chart out a vertical oval.)

Experimenting with cross-stitch patterns will help you to understand how to chart out your own motifs.

The motif and Fair Isle designs in this stitch library have all featured in various garments I have knitted, (see page 159 for contact details).

Project 8: Striped Hat

This project is perfect for practising knitting in the round, and the seamless fabric gives a neat finish on the turn-up. I usually prefer to work on a circular needle rather than double pointed needles, but as the hat is small and there are several decreases, you would stretch the stitches on a circular needle.

To Make

With 4mm (No 8/US 6) needles and Red, cast on 70 sts, dividing sts onto 3 needles. Mark end of cast on row to denote end of rounds. Work 12 rounds in st st (every round k). Cont in st st and stripe patt of 4 rounds Cream, 4 rounds Red, work 18 rounds.

Dec round [K2tog, k8] to end.
Work 3 rounds straight.
Dec round [K2tog, k7] to end.
Work 3 rounds straight.
Dec round [K2tog, k6] to end.
Work 3 rounds straight.
Dec round [K2 tog, k5] to end. 42 sts.
Work 3 rounds.
Dec round [K2 tog] to end.
Break off yarn and thread end through rem sts, pull up and secure.
With set of four 4mm (No 8/US 6) needles and Red, cast on 5 sts, dividing sts onto 3 needles. K 12 rounds. Break off yarn and thread end through sts, pull up and secure, then sew to top of hat.

Materials

1 50g ball of Rowan DK Handknit Cotton in each of Red and Cream.
Set of four 4mm (No 8/US 6) double pointed knitting needles.

Measurements

To fit 12 months old.

Tension

20 sts and 28 rows to 10cm/4in square over st st on 4mm (No 8/US 6) needles.

Abbreviations

See page 158.

Project 9: Baby Blanket

This blanket uses a combination of texture and colour with moss stitch hearts and nursery motifs. The colour patterning is worked using the intarsia technique with separate lengths of yarn for each motif.

Materials

7 50g balls of Rowan DK Handknit Cotton in Cream (A).
1 ball of same in each of Red, Blue and Yellow.
Small amount of same in each of Brown and Navy.
Pair of 4mm (No 8/US 6) knitting needles.

Measurements

Approximately 61cm x76cm/24in x 30in.

Tension

20 sts and 28 rows to 10cm/4in square over stocking stitch on 4mm (No 8/US 6) needles.

Abbreviations

See page 158.

Notes

Read charts from right to left on right side rows and from left to right on wrong side rows. When working colour motifs, use separate lengths of contrast colours for each coloured area and twist yarns together on wrong side at joins to avoid holes.

To Make

With 4mm (No 8/US 6) needles and A, cast on 123 sts.
1st row K1, [p1, k1] to end.
This row forms moss st. Moss st 3 more rows.
5th row (right side) With A, moss st 3, work 1st row of chart 1, with A, moss st 3, work 1st row of chart 2, with A, moss st 3, work 1st row of chart 1, with A, moss st 3, work 1st row of chart 3, with A, moss st 3, work 1st row of chart 1, with A, moss st 3.
6th row With A, moss st 3, work 2nd row of chart 1, with A, moss st 3, work 2nd row of chart 3, with A, moss st 3, work 2nd row of chart 1, with A, moss st 3, work 2nd row of chart 2, with A, moss st 3, work 2nd row of chart 1, with A, moss st 3.
7th to 30th rows Rep last 2 rows 12 times more but working 3rd to 26th rows of charts.
31st to 34th rows With A, rep 1st row 4 times.

35th row With A, moss st 3, work 1st row of chart 4, with A, moss st 3, work 1st row of chart 1, with A, moss st 3, work 1st row of chart 5, with A, moss st 3, work 1st row of chart 1, with A, moss st 3, work 1st row of chart 6, with A, moss st 3.
36th row With A, moss st 3, work 2nd row of chart 6, with A, moss st 3, work 2nd row of chart 1, with A, moss st 3, work 2nd row of chart 5, with A, moss st 3, work 2nd row of chart 1, with A, moss st 3, work 2nd row of chart 4, with A, moss st 3.
37th to 64th rows Work 7th to 34th rows.
65th row With A, moss st 3, work 1st row of chart 1, with A, moss st 3, work 1st row of chart 7, with A, moss st 3, work 1st row of chart 1, with A, moss st 3, work 1st row of chart 8, with A, moss st 3, work 1st row of chart 1, with A, moss st 3.
66th row With A, moss st 3, work 2nd row of chart 1, with A, moss st 3, work 2nd row of chart 8, with A, moss st 3, work 2nd row of chart 1, with A, moss st 3, work 2nd row of chart 7, with A, moss st 3, work 2nd row of chart 1, with A, moss st 3.
67th to 94th rows Work 7th to 34th rows.
95th row With A, moss st 3, work 1st row of chart 9, with A, moss st 3, work 1st row of chart 1, with A, moss st 3, work 1st row of chart 2, with A, moss st 3, work 1st row of chart 1, with A, moss st 3, work 1st row of chart 3, with A, moss st 3.
96th row With A, moss st 3, work 2nd row of chart 3, with A, moss st 3, work 2nd row of chart 1, with A, moss st 3, work 2nd row of chart 2, with A, moss st 3, work 2nd row of chart 1, with A, moss st 3, work 2nd row of chart 9, with A, moss st 3.
97th to 124th rows Work 7th to 34th rows.
125th row With A, moss st 3, work 1st row of chart 1, with A, moss st 3, work 1st row of chart 4, with A, moss st 3, work 1st row of chart 1, with A, moss st 3, work 1st row of chart 5, with A, moss st 3, work 1st row of chart 1, with A, moss st 3.
126th row With A, moss st 3, work 2nd row of chart 1, with A, moss st 3, work 2nd row of chart 5, with A, moss st 3, work 2nd row of chart 1, with A, moss st 3, work 2nd row of chart 4, with A, moss st 3, work 2nd row of chart 1, with A, moss st 3.
127th to 154th rows Work 7th to 34th rows.
155th row With A, moss st 3, work 1st row of chart 6, with A, moss st 3, work 1st row of chart 1, with A, moss st 3, work 1st row of chart 7, with A, moss st 3, work 1st

row of chart 1, with A, moss st 3, work 1st row of chart 8, with A, moss st 3.

156th row With A, moss st 3, work 2nd row of chart 8, with A, moss st 3, work 2nd row of chart 1, with A, moss st 3, work 2nd row of chart 7, with A, moss st 3, work 2nd row of chart 1, with A, moss st 3, work 2nd row of chart 6, with A, moss st 3.

157th to 184th rows Work 7th to 34th rows.

185th row With A, moss st 3, work 1st row of chart 1, with A, moss st 3, work 1st row of chart 9, with A, moss st 3, work 1st row of chart 1, with A, moss st 3, work 1st row of chart 2, with A, moss st 3, work 1st row of chart 1, with A, moss st 3.

186th row With A, moss st 3, work 2nd row of chart 1, with A, moss st 3, work 2nd row of chart 2, with A, moss st 3, work 2nd row of chart 1, with A, moss st 3, work 2nd row of chart 9, with A, moss st 3, work 2nd row of chart 1, with A, moss st 3.

187th to 214th rows Work 7th to 34 rows.
With A, cast off in moss st.
Embroider the legs and feet of each chick with straight stitches.

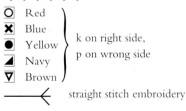

KEY FOR CHART 1

☐ with A, k on right side,
    p on wrong side

⦁ with A, p on right side,
    k on wrong side

KEY FOR CHARTS
2, 3, 4, 5, 6, 7, 8 and 9

O Red ⎫
✖ Blue ⎪
⦁ Yellow ⎬ k on right side,
◢ Navy ⎪ p on wrong side
▽ Brown ⎭

⟵ straight stitch embroidery

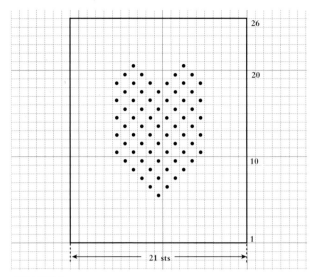

CHART 1

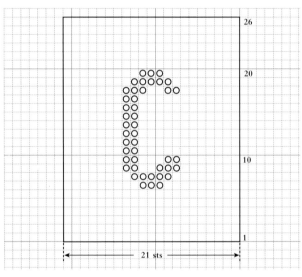

CHART 2

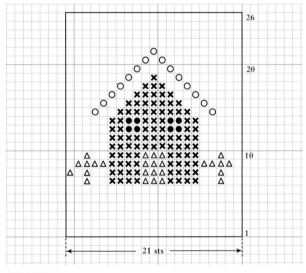

CHART 3

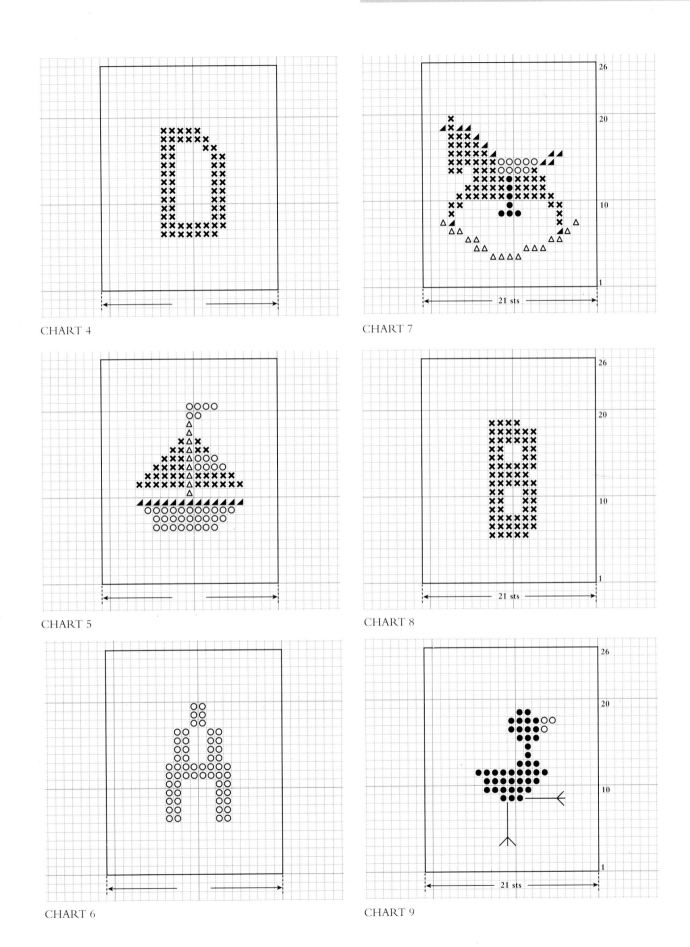

CHART 4

CHART 7

CHART 5

CHART 8

CHART 6

CHART 9

89

sts, working inc sts into patt. Cont straight until sleeve measures 48cm/19in from beg, ending with a wrong side row. Cast off.

Back Neckband

With 3mm (No 11/US 2) needles, right side facing and A, k up 8 sts down right back neck, k centre back sts, k up 8 sts up left back neck. 51(55) sts.
Beg with a 2nd row, work 6 rows in rib as given for left front. Join in B and rib 1 row. With B, cast off in rib.

Buttonhole Band

With 3mm (No 11/US 2) needles, right side facing and A, k up 100(105) sts along straight front edge of right front to beg of neck shaping and 57(62) sts along shaped edge to top of shoulder shaping. 157(167) sts.
Beg with a 2nd row, work 3 rows in rib as given for back.
Buttonhole row Rib 3, p2tog, yrn, [rib 16(18), p2tog, yrn] 5 times, rib to end.
Work a further 2 rows in rib. Join in B and rib 1 row. With B, cast off in rib.

Button Band

With 3mm (No 11/US 2) needles, right side facing and A, k up 57(62) sts down shaped edge of left front to beg of neck shaping and 100(105) sts down straight edge to cast on edge. 157(167) sts.
Beg with a 2nd row, work 6 rows in rib as given for back. Join in B and rib 1 row. With B, cast off in rib.

To Make Up (see also Finishing Workshop)

Join shoulder and band seams. Mark depth of armholes approximately 22(25)cm/8½(10)in down form shoulders at side edges of back and fronts. Sew cast off edge of sleeves between markers. Join side and sleeve seams. Sew on buttons.

KEY
☐	Cream (A)
▪	Beige
╱	Dark Green (B)
⋀	Blue
◪	Dark Pink
✖	Light Pink

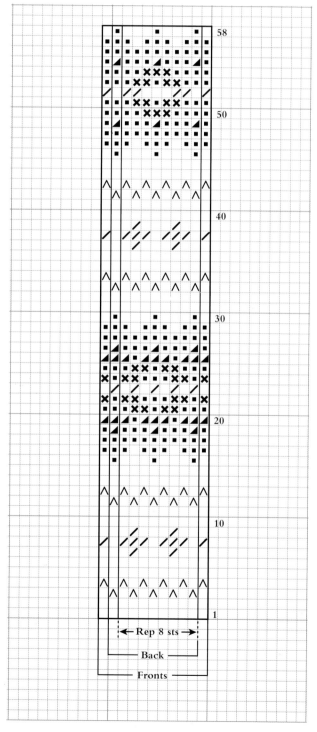

Project 11: Bright Sweater

Now you know how to work in colour, practice your Fair Isle and intarsia techniques in a child's sweater that combines both. The design has a 2-colour rib with a stocking-stitch roll.

Materials

5(6:7) 50g balls of Rowan DK Handknit Cotton in Navy (A).
2(2:3) balls of same in Royal (B).
1(1:2) balls of same in each of Lime and Pale Blue.
1 ball of same in each of Red, Pink, Lilac, Cream and Yellow.
Pair each of 3¼mm (No 10) and 4mm (No 8/US 6) knitting needles.

Measurements

To fit age	4–6	7–9	10–12	years
Actual chest	90	100	112	cm
measurement	35½	39½	44	in
Length	41	49	54	cm
	16¼	19¼	21¼	in
Sleeve seam	31	38	43	cm
	12¼	15	17	in

Tension

22 sts and 25 rows to 10cm/4in square over colour pattern on 4mm (No 8/US 6) needles.

Abbreviations

See page 158.

Notes

Read chart from right to left on right side (k) rows and from left to right on wrong side (p) rows. When working two colour rib, Fair Isle or floral bands, strand yarn not in use loosely across wrong side to keep fabric elastic. On tartan section and flower motifs, use separate lengths of contrast colours for each coloured area and twist yarns together on wrong side when changing colour to avoid holes. When working argyll part of pattern, combine the two above methods ie: strand main and diamond colours, but use short lengths of the other two diagonal colours.

Back and Front Alike

With 3¼mm (No 10/US 3) needles and A, cast on 98(110:122) sts.

Beg with a k row, work 4 rows in st st.
Join in B.
1st rib row (right side) P2A, [k2B, p2A] to end.
2nd rib row K2A, [p2B, k2A] to end.
Rep these 2 rows twice more, inc 1 st at centre of last row. 99(111:123) sts.
Change to 4mm (No 8/US 6) needles.
Beg with a k row, work in st st and colour patt from chart until 86(106:118) rows have been worked in patt.
Shape Neck
Next row Patt 38(42:46), turn.
Work on this set of sts only for first side of neck. Keeping patt correct, cast off 2 sts at beg of next row. Dec one st at neck edge on next 6 rows. 30(34:38) sts.
Shape Shoulder
Cont in A only. Cast off 15(17:19) sts at beg of next row.
Work 1 row. Cast off rem 15(17:19) sts.
With right side facing, sl centre 23(27:31) sts onto a holder, rejoin yarn to rem sts for second side of neck and patt to end. Patt 1 row. Complete to match first side of neck.

Sleeves

With 3¼mm (No 10/US 3) needles and A, cast on 46(50:54) sts.
Beg with a k row, work 4 rows in st st.
Join in B. Work 5cm/2in in two colour rib as given for back and front, ending with a 2nd row and inc 3(1:3) sts evenly across last row. 49(51:57) sts.
Change to 4mm (No 8/US 6) needles.
Beg with k row, work in st st and patt from chart, inc one st at each end of 3rd row and every foll 4th(5th:6th) row until there are 73(79:85) sts, working inc sts into patt. Patt 15(14:13) rows straight. Cast off loosely.

Neckband

Join right shoulder seam.
With 3¼mm (No 10/US 3) needles, right side facing and A, k up 10 sts down left front neck, k centre front sts, k up 10 sts up right front neck, 10 sts down right back neck, k centre back neck sts, k up 10 sts up left back neck. 86(94:102) sts.
Join in B and beg with a 2nd row, work two colour rib as given for back and front for 4 rows. Cont in A only.
Beg with a p row, work 4 rows in st st. Cast off loosely purlwise.

To Make Up (see also Finishing Workshop)

Join left shoulder and neckband seam, reversing seam on
st st section of neckband. Mark depth of armholes
approximately 17(18:19)cm/6¾(7:7½)in down from
shoulders at side edges of back and front. Sew cast off
edge of sleeves between markers. Join side and sleeve
seams, reversing seam on first and last 4 rows.

KEY

☐	Navy (A)
▪	Royal (B)
◯	Lime
◢	Pale Blue
✖	Red
△	Pink
⋁	Lilac
⊟	Cream
◸	Yellow
●	with Cream make bobble: k into front, back, front and back of next st, pass 2nd, 3rd and 4th st over 1st st.

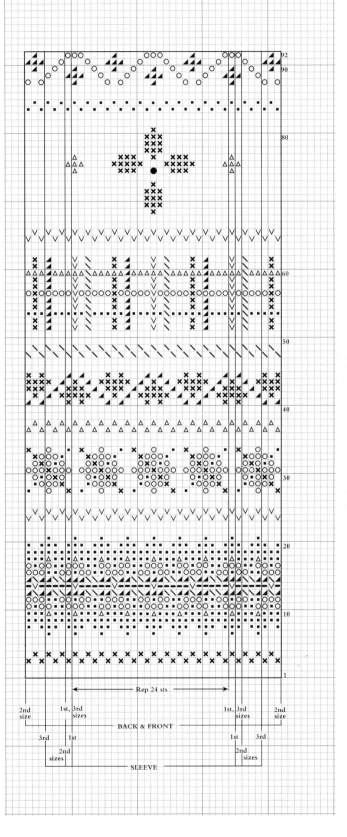

95

CHAPTER FIVE

Lace Workshop

I AVOIDED LACE KNITTING for a long time, telling myself that the delicate patterns were not really my style. In reality, however, I was intimidated by it, convinced that it was too intricate for me to tackle. It was a relief, therefore, to discover that there were plenty of 'starter' lace patterns and that the basic principle was the same for both the simple and the more complicated varieties. As I gained confidence I realised that not only were many of the patterns quite beautiful but that, used as an edging on a collar or cuff, or added between cables to introduce a lighter note, they could really make the most of a simple design.

The first of the two projects in this workshop is a lace edging that can be used on a garment as well as a trim for a pillowcase or tablecloth, or as the shelf edging shown here. The second project is a lace tunic with a pretty scalloped edge that is very simple to work. Like most lace designs, the tunic benefits from being knitted in a fine cotton that shows up the stitch.

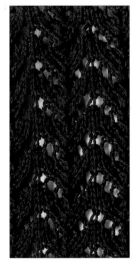

Practice the more complicated stitches from the stitch library (see pages 102–109) and you will find that the basic technique stays pretty much the same, with the holes always being formed by taking the yarn over the needle.

Yarn Overs

Here, stitches and holes are created by making loops around the needle, these are known as yarn overs. The examples given are between single stitches, but the stitch following the loop can vary.

Yarn Round Needle (yrn)

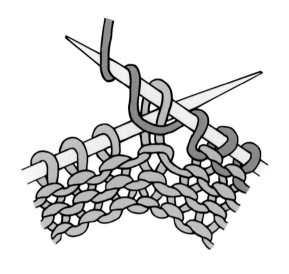

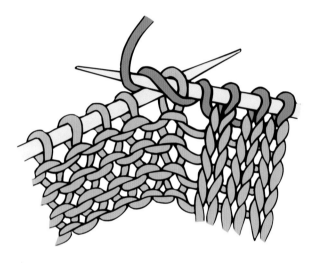

This is worked between two purl stitches. Take the yarn over the top of the right-hand needle and under the needle to the front again then purl the next stitch.

This is worked between a knit and a purl stitch. Bring the yarn forward under the right-hand needle, over the top of the needle to the back and under the needle to the front then purl the next stitch.

Yarn Forward (yf)

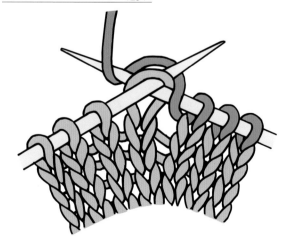

This is worked between two knit stitches. Bring the yarn forward under the right-hand needle, then knit the next stitch taking the yarn over the top of the needle to do so.

Yarn Over Needle (yon)

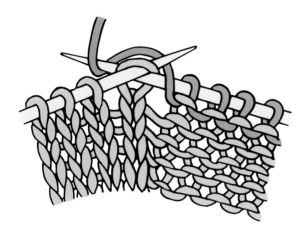

This is worked between a purl and a knit stitch. Take the yarn over the top of the right-hand needle then knit the next stitch.

TIPS: LACE

Yarn overs are most commonly used in lace patterns where you are creating a hole by making up stitches where some have been lost by working them together. The way the yarn is taken over the needle depends on the stitches on either side of the hole – whether they have been knitted, purled, or a combination of both.

Complications often arise when a lace pattern is shaped at the sides. Unless row-by-row instructions are given the knitter needs to really concentrate to keep the lace pattern correct. I find that the following helps. In most lace patterns for every eyelet or hole there is also a decrease. When shaping, regard these as pairs and do not work an eyelet without having enough stitches to work the decrease and vice versa. Check at the end of every row that you have the correct number of stitches and that the eyelets and decreases are in position above the previous pattern row. If there are insufficient stitches to work the eyelet and the decrease, then work the end stitches in the background fabric. When the shaping only needs a small decrease, insert a marker at the end of the first pattern repeat in from the edge. At the end of every decrease row check that there is the correct number of stitches in the marked sections.

Yarn Round Needle Twice

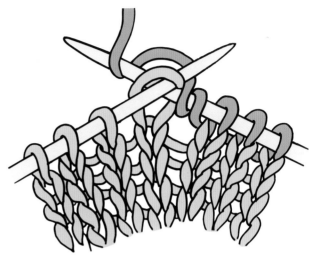

This is worked between two knit stitches. Bring the yarn forward under the right-hand needle, over the top of the needle and under the needle to the front again, then over the top of the needle to knit the next stitch.

Above *Strong colours or neutrals can give a touch of sophistication to lace patterns while some pastel shades may introduce an undesirable 'bedjacket' look. This detail is from Project 13: Lacy Tunic (see page 112 for pattern instructions).*

Additional Decreases

In addition to the simple decrease (see page 20) there are the slightly more complex shaping methods shown here which are required for some shapes and stitch patterns.

Knit Three Together (k3tog)

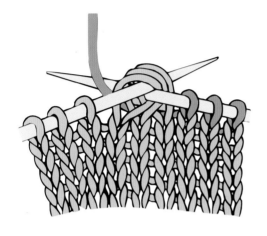

Insert the right-hand needle from left to right through the front of the three stitches then knit them together as one stitch.

Purl Three Together (p3tog)

Insert the right-hand needle from right to left through front of the three stitches then purl them together as one stitch.

Knit Two Together Through Back Of Loops (k2tog tbl)

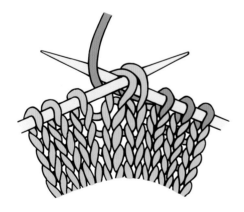

This is similar to k2tog (see page 20), but the stitches are knitted together through the back of the loops, thus twisting them. Insert the right-hand needle from right to left through the back of the two stitches, then knit them together as one stitch.

Purl Two Together Through Back Of Loops (p2tog tbl)

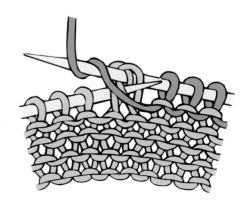

On a purl row the stitches are purled together through the back of the loops, which is a little awkward to work. Insert the right-hand needle from left to right through the back of the two stitches, then purl them together as one stitch.

Slip One, Knit One, Pass Slipped Stitch Over (sl1-k1-psso or skpo)

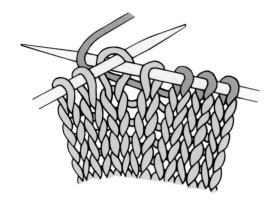

1 Insert the right-hand needle knitwise into the first stitch, slip this stitch onto the right-hand needle without knitting it, then knit the next stitch.

2 Using the left-hand needle, lift the slipped stitch over the knitted stitch and off the needle. This whole process is often abbreviated to 'skpo'.

Slip One, Knit Two Together, Pass Slipped Stitch Over (sl1-k2tog-psso)

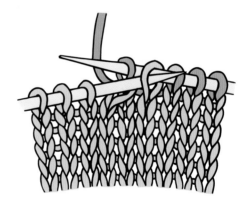

1 Insert the right-hand needle knitwise into the first stitch and slip this stitch onto the right-hand needle without knitting it, then knit the next two stitches together.

2 Using the left-hand needle, lift the slipped stitch over the stitch just made and off the needle.

TIPS: DECREASING

Usually when a pattern tells you to decrease stitches you can just use the simple method (see page 20). But in some circumstances, particularly when the shaping will be visible on the finished design and when it does, therefore, needs to look attractive and so should be symmetrical, the pattern will instruct you to use one of the methods shown on these two pages. Under these circumstances, do resist the temptation to use the simple decrease method instead, it will only make your finished piece of knitting look untidy.

Lace Stitch Library

This stitch library guides you through very simple lace eyelet patterns and on to more complicated ones that combine lace with other techniques such as cabling. Also included are some panel patterns that can be worked into an otherwise plain garment.

Chevron And Feather

Multiple of 13 sts + 1 st.
1st row (right side) K1, [yf, k4, k2tog, skpo, k4, yf, k1] to end.
2nd row Purl to end.
Rep these 2 rows.

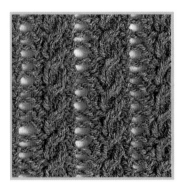

Twist Cable And Ladder Lace

Multiple of 7 sts + 6 sts.
1st row (right side) K1, [k2tog, yf and around needle thus making 2 sts, skpo, k3] to last 5 sts, k2tog, yf and around needle, skpo, k1.
2nd row K2, [k in front and back into yf and around needle of previous row, k1, p3, k1] to last 4 sts, k in front and back into yf and around needle of previous row, k2.
3rd row K1, [k2tog, yf and around needle, skpo, knit into front of 3rd st on left-hand needle, then knit into 2nd st, then knit 1st st, slipping all 3 sts off left-hand needle tog] to last 5 sts, k2tog, yf and

around needle, skpo, k1.
4th row As 2nd row.
Rep these 4 rows.

Eyelets

Multiple of 3 sts + 2 sts.
1st row (right side) K to end.
2nd row P to end
3rd row K2, [yf, k2tog, k1] to end.
4th row Purl to end.
Rep these 4 rows.

Chevron Rib

Multiple of 7 sts + 2 sts.
1st row (right side) K2, [k2tog, yf, k1, yf, skpo, k2] to end.
2nd row Purl to end.
3rd row K1, [k2tog, yf, k3, yf, skpo] to last st, k1.
4th row Purl to end.
Rep these 4 rows.

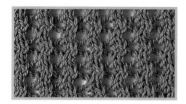

Faggotting

Multiple of 3 sts.

Note: number of sts varies on some rows.

1st row (right side) [K1, yf and around needle thus making 2 loops, k2tog] to end.

2nd row P1, [purl into yf and around needle of previous row, dropping extra loop off needle, p2] to last 3 sts, purl into yf and around needle of previous row, dropping extra loop off needle, p1.

3rd row [K2tog, yf and around needle, k1] to end.

4th row As 2nd row.

Rep these 4 rows.

Scallop Pattern

Multiple of 13 sts + 2 sts.

Note: due to the nature of the pattern the number of sts varies on some rows and they should only be counted after the 5th or 6th row of the pattern.

1st row (right side) K1, [skpo, k9, k2tog] to last st, k1.

2nd row Purl to end.

3rd row K1, [skpo, k7, k2tog] to last st, k1.

4th row Purl to end.

5th row K1, *skpo, yf, [k1, yf] 5 times, k2tog; rep from * to last st, k1.

6th row Knit to end.

Rep these 6 rows.

Feather And Fan

Multiple of 18 sts + 2 sts.

1st row (right side) Knit to end.

2nd row Purl to end.

3rd row K1, *[k2tog] 3 times, [yf, k1] 6 times, [k2tog] 3 times; rep from * to last st, k1.

4th row Knit to end.

Rep these 4 rows.

Two-coloured Feather And Fan

Worked as **Feather And Fan**.

Work 4 rows in colour A and 4 rows in colour B throughout.

Cell Stitch

Multiple of 4 sts + 3 sts.

1st row (right side) K2, [yf, sl 1, k2tog, psso, yf, k1] to last st, k1.

2nd row Purl to end.

3rd row K1, k2tog, yf, k1, [yf, sl 1, k2tog, psso, yf, k1] to last 3 sts, yf, skpo, k1.

4th row Purl to end.

Rep these 4 rows.

Feather Lace

Multiple of 6 sts + 1 st.

1st row (right side) K1, [yf, k2tog tbl, k1, k2tog, yf, k1] to end.

2nd and every alt row Purl to end.

3rd row K1, [yf, k1, sl 1, k2tog, psso, k1, yf, k1] to end.

5th row K1, [k2tog, yf, k1, yf, k2tog tbl, k1] to end.

7th row K2tog, ★[k1, yf] twice, k1, sl 1, k2tog, psso; rep from ★ to last 5 sts, [k1, yf] twice, k1, k2tog tbl.

8th row Purl to end.

Rep these 8 rows.

Horseshoe Print

Multiple of 10 sts + 1 st.

1st row (wrong side) Purl to end.

2nd row K1, [yf, k3, sl 1, k2tog, psso, k3, yf, k1] to end.

3rd row Purl to end.

4th row P1, [k1, yf, k2, sl 1, k2tog, psso, k2, yf, k1, p1] to end.

5th row K1, [p9, k1] to end.

6th row P1, [k2, yf, k1, sl 1, k2tog, psso, k1, yf, k2, p1] to end.

7th row As 5th row.

8th row P1, [k3, yf, sl 1, k2tog, psso, yf, k3, p1] to end.

Rep these 8 rows.

Diagonal Openwork

Multiple of 4 sts + 2 sts.

1st row (right side) [K1, yf, sl 1, k2tog, psso, yf] to last 2 sts, k2.

2nd and every alt row Purl to end.

3rd row K2, [yf, sl 1, k2tog, psso, yf, k1] to end.

5th row K2tog, yf, k1, [yf, sl 1, k2tog, psso, yf, k1] to last 3 sts, yf, skpo, k1.

7th row K1, k2tog, yf, k1, [yf, sl 1, k2tog, psso, yf, k1] to last 2 sts, yf, skpo.

8th row Purl to end.

Rep these 8 rows.

Cascading Leaves

Panel of 14 sts on background of reverse st st.

1st row (right side) K3, k2tog, k1, yrn, p2, yon, k1, skpo, k3.

2nd and every alt row P6, k2, p6.

3rd row K2, k2tog, k1, yf, k1, p2, k1, yf, k1, skpo, k2.

5th row K1, k2tog, k1, yf, k2, p2, k2, yf, k1, skpo, k1.

7th row K2tog, k1, yf, k3, p2, k3, yf, k1, skpo.

8th row P6, k2, p6.

Rep these 8 rows.

Eyelet Chevron

Multiple of 12 sts + 1 st.

1st row (right side) K4, [k2tog, yf, k1, yf, skpo, k7] to last 9 sts, k2tog, yf, k1, yf, skpo, k4.

2nd and every alt row Purl to end.

3rd row K3, [k2tog, yf, k3, yf, skpo, k5] to last 10 sts, k2tog, yf, k3, yf, skpo, k3.

5th row K2, [k2tog, yf, k5, yf, skpo, k3] to last 11 sts, k2tog, yf, k5, yf, skpo, k2.

7th row K1, [k2tog, yf, k7, yf, skpo, k1] to end

9th row K2tog, yf, k9, [yf, sl 1, k2tog, psso, yf, k9] to last 2 sts, yf, skpo.

10th row Purl to end.

Rep these 10 rows.

Loose Lattice Lace

Multiple of 8 sts + 3 sts.

Note: due to the nature of the pattern the number of sts varies on some rows and should only be counted after the 5th, 6th, 11th and 12th rows.

1st row (right side) K1, [k2tog, k1, yf, k1, skpo, k2] to last 2 sts, k2.

2nd and every alt row Purl to end.

3rd row *K2tog, k1, [yf, k1] twice, skpo; rep from * to last 3 sts, k3.

5th row K2, [yf, k3, yf, k1, skpo, k1] to last st, k1.

7th row K4, [k2tog, k1, yf, k1, skpo, k2] to last 7 sts, k2tog, k1, yf, k1, skpo, k1.

9th row K3, *k2tog, k1, [yf, k1] twice, skpo; rep from * to end.

11th row K2, [k2tog, k1, yf, k3, yf, k1] to last st, k1.

12th row Purl to end.

Rep these 12 rows.

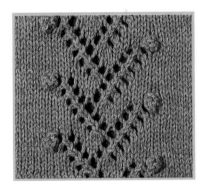

Eyelet Twigs And Bobbles

Panel of 16 st on background of st st.

Special abbreviation: mb = make 3 st bobble thus: knit into front, back and front of next st, turn and k3, turn, p3, turn, k3, turn and sl 1, k2tog, psso.

1st row (right side) K2, yf, k3tog, yf, k3, yf, sl 1, k2tog, psso, yf, k5.

2nd and every alt row Purl to end.

3rd row K1, yf, k3tog, yf, k5, yf, sl 1, k2tog, psso, yf, k4.

5th row Mb, k5, yf, k3tog, yf, k1, yf, sl 1, k2tog, psso, yf, k3.

7th row K5, yf, k3tog, yf, k3, yf, sl 1, k2tog, psso, yf, k2.

9th row K4, yf, k3tog, yf, k5, yf, sl 1, k2tog, psso, yf, mb.

11th row K3, yf, k3tog, yf, k1, yf, sl 1, k2tog, psso, yf, k6.

12th row Purl to end.

Rep these 12 rows.

Zigzag Panel

Panel of 9 sts on background of st st.

1st row (right side) K3, skpo, yf, k2tog, yf, k2.

2nd and every alt row Purl to end.

3rd row K2, skpo, yf, k2tog, yf, k3.

5th row K1, skpo, yf, k2tog, yf, k4.

7th row Skpo, yf, k2tog, yf, k5.

9th row K2, yf, skpo, yf, k2tog, k3.

11th row K3, yf, skpo, yf, k2tog, k2,

13th row K4, yf, skpo, yf, k2tog, k1.

15th row K5, yf, skpo, yf, k2tog.

16th row Purl to end.

Rep these 16 rows.

Falling Leaves

Multiple of 10 sts +3 sts.

1st row (right side) K1, k2tog, k3, [yf, k1, yf, k3, sl 1, k2tog, psso, k3] to last 7 sts, yf, k1, yf, k3, skpo, k1.

2nd and every alt row Purl to end.

3rd row K1, k2tog, k2, [yf, k3, yf, k2, sl 1, k2tog, psso, k2] to last 8 sts, yf, k3, yf, k2, skpo, k1.

5th row K1, k2tog, k1, [yf, k5, yf, k1, sl 1, k2tog, psso, k1] to last 9 sts, yf, k5, yf, k1, skpo, k1.

7th row K1, k2tog, yf, k7, [yf, sl 1, k2tog, psso, yf, k7] to last 3 sts, yf, skpo, k1.

9th row K2, yf, k3, [sl 1, k2tog, psso, k3, yf, k1, yf, k3] to last 8 sts, sl 1, k2tog, psso, k3, yf, k2.

11th row K3, [yf, k2, sl 1, k2tog, psso, k2, yf, k3] to end.

13th row K4, yf, k1, [sl 1, k2tog, psso, k1, yf, k5, yf, k1] to last 8 sts, yf, sl 1, k2tog, psso, k1, yf, k4.

15th row K5, [yf, sl 1, k2tog, psso, yf, k7] to last 8 sts, yf, sl 1, k2tog, psso, yf, k5.

16th row Purl to end.

Rep these 16 rows.

Ears Of Corn

Multiple of 12 sts + 2 sts.

1st row (right side) Knit to end.

2nd row Purl to end.

3rd row K4, k2tog, k1, yf, [k9, k2tog, k1, yf] to last 7 sts, k7.

4th row P8, yrn, p1, p2tog, [p9, yrn, p1, p2tog] to last 3 sts, p3.

5th row K2, [k2tog, k1, yf, k9] to end.

6th row P10, yrn, p1, p2tog, [p9, yrn, p1, p2tog] to last st, p1.

7th and 8th rows As 1st and 2nd rows.

9th row K7, yf, k1, skpo, [k9, yf, k1, skpo] to last 4 sts, k4.

10th row P3, p2tog tbl, p1, yrn, [p9, p2tog tbl, p1, yrn] to last 8 sts, p8.

11th row [K9, yf, k1, skpo] to last 2 sts, k2.

12th row P1, p2tog tbl, p1, yrn, [p9, p2tog tbl, p1, yrn] to last 10 sts, p10.
Rep these 12 rows.

Diamond Lace

Multiple of 6 sts + 3 sts.
1st row (right side) [K4, yf, skpo] to last 3 sts, k3.
2nd and every alt row Purl to end.
3rd row K2, [k2tog, yf, k1, yf, skpo, k1] to last st, k1.
5th row K1, k2tog, yf, k3, [yf, sl 1, k2tog, psso, yf, k3] to last 3 sts, yf, skpo, k1.
7th row K3, [yf, sl 1, k2tog, psso, yf, k3] to end.
9th row As 1st row.
11th row K1, [yf, skpo, k4] to last 2 sts, yf, skpo.
13th row K2, [yf, skpo, k1, k2tog, yf, k1] to last st, k1.
15th row As 7th row.
17th row As 5th row.
19th row As 11th row.
20th row Purl to end.
Rep these 20 rows.

Fern Diamonds

Multiple of 10 sts + 1 st.
1st row (right side) K3, [k2tog, yf, k1, yf, skpo, k5] to last 8 sts, k2tog, yf, k1, yf, skpo, k3.
2nd and every alt row Purl to end.
3rd row K2, *k2tog, [k1, yf] twice, k1, skpo, k3; rep from * to last 9 sts, k2tog, [k1, yf] twice, k1, skpo, k2.
5th row K1, [k2tog, k2, yf, k1, yf, k2, skpo, k1] to end.
7th row K2tog, [k3, yf, k1, yf, k3, sl 1, k2tog, psso] to last 9 sts, k3, yf, k1, yf, k3, skpo.
9th row K1, [yf, skpo, k5, k2tog, yf, k1] to end.
11th row K1, [yf, k1, skpo, k3, k2tog, k1, yf, k1] to end.
13th row K1, [yf, k2, skpo, k1, k2tog, k2, yf, k1] to end.
15th row K1, [yf, k3, sl 1, k2tog, psso, k3, yf, k1] to end.
16th row Purl to end.
Rep these 16 rows.

Tulip Bud Motif

Worked over 33 sts on background of garter st.

Note: due to the nature of the pattern the number of sts within the motif varies on some rows.

1st row (wrong side) K16, p1, k16.
2nd row K14, k2tog, yf, k1, yf, skpo, k14.
3rd row K14, p5, k14.
4th row K13, k2tog, yf, k3, yf, skpo, k13.
5th row K13, p7, k13.
6th row K12, [k2tog, yf] twice, k1, [yf, skpo] twice, k12.
7th row K12, p9, k12.
8th row K11, [k2tog, yf] twice, k3, [yf, skpo] twice, k11.
9th row K11, p4, k1, p1, k1, p4, k11.
10th row K10, [k2tog, yf] twice, k5, [yf, skpo] twice, k10.
11th row K10, p4, k2, p1, k2, p4, k10.
12th row K9, [k2tog, yf] twice, k3, yf, k1, yf, k3, [yf, skpo] twice, k9. 35 sts.
13th row K9, p4, k3, p3, k3, p4, k9.
14th row K1, yf, skpo, k5, [k2tog, yf] twice, k5, yf, k1, yf, k5, [yf, skpo] twice, k5, k2tog, yf, k1. 37 sts.
15th row K1, p2, k5, p4, k4, p5, k4, p4, k5, p2, k1.
16th row K2, yf, skpo, k3, [k2tog, yf] twice, k7, yf, k1, yf, k7, [yf, skpo] twice, k3, k2tog, yf, k2. 39 sts.
17th row K2, p2, k3, p4, k5, p7, k5, p4, k3, p2, k2.
18th row K3, yf, skpo, k1, [k2tog, yf] twice, k9, yf, k1, yf, k9, [yf, skpo] twice, k1, k2tog, yf, k3. 41 sts.
19th row K3, p2, k1, p4, k6, p9, k6, p4, k1, p2, k3.
20th row K4, yf, sl 1, k2tog, psso, yf, k2tog, yf, k7, skpo, k5, k2tog, k7, yf, skpo, yf, k3tog, yf, k4. 39sts.
21st row K4, p5, k7, p7, k7, p5, k4.
22nd row K16, skpo, k3, k2tog, k16. 37 sts.
23rd row K16, p5, k16.
24th row K16, skpo, k1, k2tog, k16. 35 sts.
25th row K16, p3, k16.
26th row K16, sl 1, k2tog, psso, k16. 33sts.
27th row As 1st row.

Meandering Cable With Eyelets

Multiple of 16 sts + 10 sts.

Note: the number of sts varies and should only be counted after the 1st, 14th, 15th and 28th rows. (See also abbreviations for Aran Stitch Library, page 158.)

1st row (wrong side) K2, [p6, k2] to end.
2nd row P2, [k2tog, yf] twice, k2tog, *p2, k6, p2, [k2tog, yf] twice, k2tog; rep from * to last 2 sts, p2.
3rd row K2, p5, k2, [p6, k2, p5, k2] to end.
4th row P2, k1, [yf, k2tog] twice, p2, *C6F, p2, k1, [yf, k2tog] twice, p2, rep from * to end.
5th row As 3rd row.
6th row P2, k1, [yf, k2tog] twice, p2, *k6, p2, k1, [yf, k2tog] twice, p2; rep from * to end.
7th to 11th rows Rep 5th and 6th rows twice more, then the 5th row again.
12th row As 4th row.
13th row As 3rd row.
14th row P2, k2, yf, k1, yf, k2tog, p2, [k6, p2, k2, yf, k1, yf, k2tog, p2] to end.
15th row As 1st row.
16th row P2, k6, p2, *yb, skpo, [yf, skpo] twice, p2, k6, p2; rep from * to end.
17th row K2, p6, k2, [p5, k2, p6, k2] to end.
18th row P2, C6F, p2, *yb, [skpo, yf] twice, k1, p2, C6F, p2; rep from * to end.
19th row As 17th row.
20th row P2, k6, p2, *yb, [skpo, yf] twice, k1, p2, k6, p2; rep from * to end.
21st to 25th rows Rep 19th and 20th rows twice more, then 19th row again.
26th and 27th rows As 18th and 19th rows.
28th row P2, k6, p2, [k2, yf, skpo, yf, k1, p2, k6, p2] to end.

Rep these 28 rows.

Ornamental Parasols

Multiple of 18 sts + 1 st.

Note: the number of sts varies on some rows and should only be counted after the 5th, 6th, 11th, 12th, 13th, 14th, 19th, 20th, 25th, 26th, 27th and 28th rows.

1st row (right side) K1, *[p2, k1] twice, yf, k2tog, yf, k1, yf, skpo, yf, [k1, p2] twice, k1; rep from * to end.

2nd row [P1, k2] twice, p9, *k2, [p1, k2] 3 times, p9; rep from * to last 6 sts, [k2, p1] twice.

3rd row K1, *[p2, k1] twice, yf, k2tog, yf, k3, yf, skpo, yf, [k1, p2] twice, k1; rep from * to end.

4th row [P1, k2] twice, p11, *k2, [p1, k2] 3 times, p11; rep from * to last 6 sts, [k2, p1] twice.

5th row K1, *[p2tog, k1] twice, yf, k2tog, yf, skpo, k1, k2tog, yf, skpo, yf, [k1, p2tog] twice, k1; rep from * to end.

6th row [P1, k1] twice, p11, *k1, [p1, k1] 3 times, p11; rep from * to last 4 sts, [k1, p1] twice.

7th row K1, *[p1, k1] twice, yf, k2tog, yf, k1 tbl, yf, sl 1, k2tog, psso, yf, k1 tbl, yf, skpo, yf, [k1, p1] twice, k1; rep from * to end.

8th row [P1, k1] twice, p13, *k1, [p1, k1] 3 times, p13; rep from * to last 4 sts, [k1, p1] twice.

9th row K1, *[k2tog] twice, yf, k2tog, yf, k3, yf, k1, yf, k3, yf, skpo, yf, [skpo] twice, k1; rep from * to end.

10th row Purl to end.

11th row K1, *[k2tog, yf] twice, skpo, k1, k2tog, yf, k1, yf, skpo, k1, k2tog, [yf, skpo] twice, k1; rep from * to end.

12th row Purl to end.

13th row [K2tog, yf] twice, k1 tbl, yf, sl 1, k2tog, psso, yf, k3, yf, sl 1, k2tog, psso, yf, k1 tbl, yf, skpo, *yf, sl 1, k2tog, psso, yf, k2tog, yf, k1 tbl, yf, sl 1, k2tog, psso, yf, k3, yf, sl 1, k2tog, psso, yf, k1 tbl, yf, skpo; rep from * to last 2 sts, yf, skpo.

14th row Purl to end.

15th row K1, *yf, skpo, yf, [k1, p2] 4 times, k1, yf, k2tog, yf, k1; rep from * to end.

16th row P5, [k2, p1] 3 times, k2, *p9, [k2, p1] 3 times, k2; rep from * to last 5 sts, p5.

17th row K2, yf, skpo, yf, [k1, p2] 4 times, k1, yf, k2tog, *yf, k3, yf, skpo, yf, [k1, p2] 4 times, k1, yf, k2tog; rep from * to last 2 sts, yf, k2.

18th row P6, [k2, p1] 3 times, k2, *p11, [k2, p1] 3 times, k2; rep from * to last 6 sts, p6.

19th row K1, *k2tog, yf, skpo, yf, [k1, p2tog] 4 times, k1, yf, k2tog, yf, skpo, k1; rep from * to end.

20th row P6, [k1, p1] 3 times, k1, * p11, [k1, p1] 3 times, k1; rep from * to last 6 sts, p6.

21st row K2tog, yf, k1 tbl, yf, skpo, yf, [k1, p1] 4 times, k1, yf, k2tog, yf, k1 tbl, * yf, sl 1, k2tog, psso, yf, k1 tbl, yf, skpo, yf, [k1, p1] 4 times, k1, yf, k2tog, yf, k1 tbl; rep from * to last 2 sts, yf, skpo.

22nd row P7, [k1, p1] 3 times, k1, *p13, [k1, p1] 3 times, k1; rep from * to last 7 sts, p7.

23rd row K1, * yf, k3, yf, skpo, yf, [skpo] twice, k1, [k2tog] twice, yf, k2tog, yf, k3, yf, k1; rep from * to end.

24th row Purl to end.

25th row K1, *yf, skpo, k1, k2tog, [yf, skpo] twice, k1, [k2tog, yf] twice, skpo, k1, k2tog, yf, k1; rep from * to end.

26th row Purl to end.

27th row K2, yf, sl 1, k2tog, psso, yf, k1 tbl, yf, skpo, yf, sl 1, k2tog, psso, yf, k2tog, yf, k1 tbl, yf, sl 1, k2tog, psso, *yf, k3, yf, sl 1, k2tog, psso, yf, k1 tbl, yf, skpo, yf, sl 1, k2tog, psso, yf, k2tog, yf, k1 tbl, yf, sl 1, k2tog, psso; rep from * to last 2 sts, yf, k2.

28th row Purl to end.

Rep these 28 rows.

Project 12: Lace Edging

This pretty edging is formed by a simple 16-row repeat which looks harder to knit than it really is.

Materials

Allow 1 50g ball of Rowan 4 ply Cotton for approximately 8 metres/9 yards of edging.
Pair of 3¼ mm (No 10/US 3) knitting needles.

Tension

2 pattern repeats measure approximately 9cm/3½in long.

Abbreviations

See page 158.

Method

With 3¼ mm (No 10/US 3) needles cast on 5 sts.
1st row K1, yf, k2tog, yf, k2. 6 sts.
2nd row and every alt row K.
3rd row K1, [yf, k2tog] twice, yf, k1. 7 sts.
5th row K1, [yf, k2tog] twice, yf, k2. 8 sts.
7th row K1, [yf, k2tog] 3 times, yf, k1. 9 sts.
9th row K1, [yf, k2tog] 3 times, yf, k2. 10 sts.
11th row K1, [yf, k2tog] 4 times, yf, k1. 11 sts.
13th row K1, [yf, k2tog] 4 times, yf, k2. 12 sts.
15th row Cast off 8 sts, 1 st on right hand needle, yf, k2tog, yf, k1. 5 sts.
16th row K.
These 16 rows form pattern. Rep these 16 rows until required length, ending with 15th row. Cast off.

Project 13: Lacy Tunic

With only a 6-row repeat this simple but elegant tunic has an easy-to-follow lace pattern which forms a scalloped hem. The front and back are the same, creating a scooped neck.

Materials

8(9:10) 50g balls of Rowan 4 ply Cotton.
Pair each of 3mm (No 11/US 2) and 3¼mm (No 10/US 3) knitting needles.

Measurements

To fit bust	86	91	98	cm
	34	36	38	in
Actual bust	103	109	116	cm
measurement	40½	43	45½	in
Length	68	70	72	cm
	26¾	27¾	28½	in
Sleeve seam	44	46	46	cm
	17¼	18	18	in

Tension

25 sts and 32 rows to 10cm/4in square over pattern on 3¼mm (No 10/US 3) needles.

Abbreviations

See page 158.

Back and Front Alike

With 3mm (No 11/US 2) needles cast on 129(137:145) sts.
K 3 rows.
Change to 3¼mm (No 10/US 3) needles.
1st row (right side) K1, [yf, k2, sl 1, k2 tog, psso, k2, yf, k1] to end.
2nd and 4th rows P.
3rd row K2, [yf, k1, sl 1, k2 tog, psso, k1, yf, k3] to last 7 sts, yf, k1, sl 1, k2tog, psso, k1, yf, k2.
5th row K3, [yf, sl 1, k2 tog, psso, yf, k5] to last 6 sts, yf, sl 1, k2 tog, psso, yf, k3.
6th row P.
These 6 rows form patt. Cont in patt until work measures 62.5(64.5:66.5)cm/24½(25½:26¼)in from beg, ending with 6th row of patt.
Shape Neck
Next row Patt 38(41: 46), turn.
Work on this set of sts for first side of neck. Keeping patt correct, dec one st at neck edge on next 2 rows, then on 6 foll alt rows. 30(33:38) sts. Work 3 rows.

Cast off loosely.
With right side facing, sl centre 53(55:53) sts onto a holder, rejoin yarn to rem sts for second side of neck and patt to end. Complete as given for first side of neck.

Sleeves

With 3mm (No 11/US 2) needles cast on 49(49:57) sts.
K 3 rows.
Change to 3¼mm (No 10/US 3) needles.
Work in patt as given for back and front, inc one st at each end of 7th row and every foll 4th row until there are 97(109:117) sts, working inc sts into patt. Cont straight until sleeve measures 44(46:46)cm/17¼(18:18)in from beg, ending with a wrong side row. Cast off loosely.

Neckband

Join right shoulder seam.
With 3mm (No 11/US 2) needles and right side facing, k up 15 sts down left side of front neck, work across centre front sts as follows: k9(7:9), [k2tog, k9(6:9)] 4(6:4) times, k up 15 sts up right side of front neck, 15 sts down right side of back neck, work across centre back sts as follows: k9(7:9). [k2 tog, k9(6:9)] 4(6:4) times, k up 15 sts up left side of back neck. 158 sts. K 3 rows.
Cast off knitwise.

To Make Up (see also Finishing Workshop)

Join left shoulder and neckband seam. Mark depth of armholes approximately 20(22:23)cm/8(8½:9)in down from shoulders at side edges of back and front. Sew cast off edge of sleeves between markers. Join side and sleeve seams.

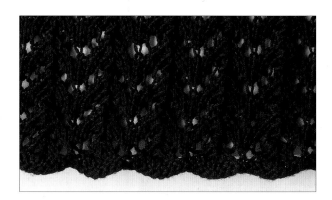

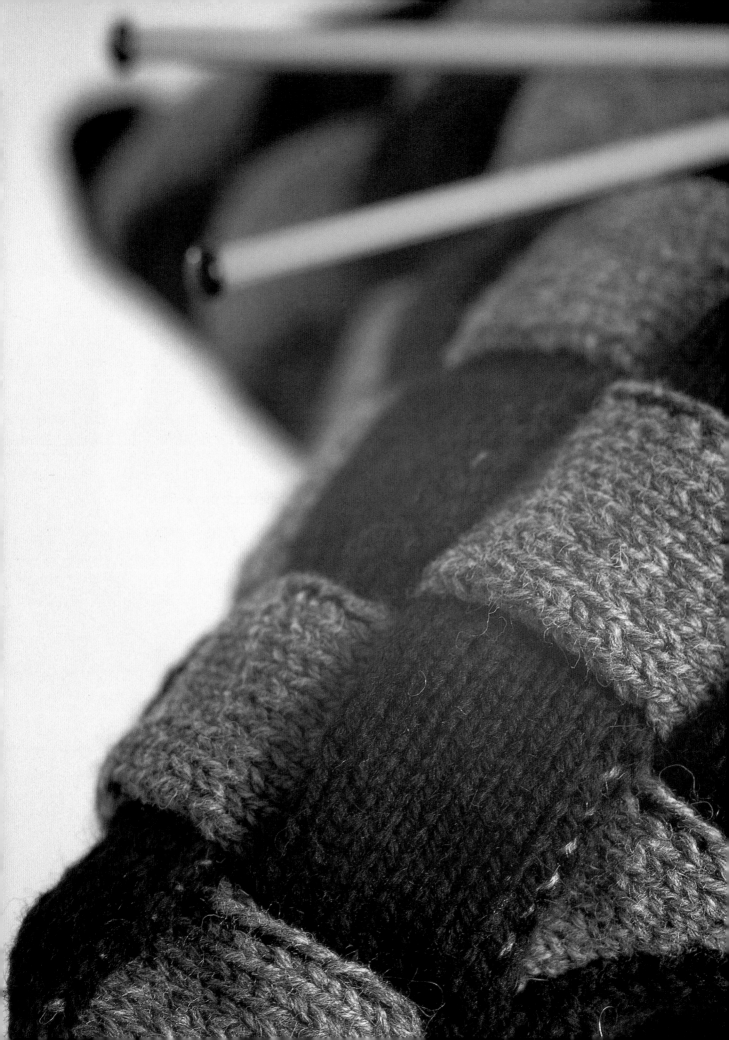

CHAPTER SIX

Entrelac Workshop

I WAS FIRST INTRODUCED to entrelac at a show organised by *Knitters Magazine* in San Francisco. I had seen examples of it before worked in colour but had not felt particularly inspired by the effect. However, at the show I saw a wonderful jacket that had appeared in the publication, worked in texture rather than colour and I could not wait to get my hands on a pair of needles and get started. Luckily for me I was introduced to the designer, Bette Ann Lampers of Snohomish, W.A. who sat me down and patiently showed me the basic technique, even though she was in grave danger of missing her plane home.

Entrelac (it originates from the French *entrelacer* which means to interlace) creates a diagonal patchwork effect, worked in rectangles in rows rather than individually. Each area is worked from the previous row of rectangles and becomes the base of the next. Personally I feel that the only way to really understand how it works is to knit a sample and then the logic of the technique will fall into place.

With this in mind, the first step is to knit a plain stocking stitch sample in one colour. Then, with the basic principle established, the following two projects introduce two-colour and textured entrelac designs.

Entrelac Technique

This technique is difficult to illustrate: when you read the pattern you will realise that the stitches remain on the needle. However, if it were drawn that way the work would be bunched up on the needle and you would not see what is happening. So read the instructions carefully and all will be clear.

Cast on very loosely 40 sts.

Work base triangles as follows:

First base triangle

1st and 2nd rows K2, turn, p2, turn.
3rd and 4th rows K3, turn, p3, turn.
5th and 6th rows K4, turn, p4, turn.
7th and 8th rows K5, turn, p5, turn.
9th and 10th rows K6, turn, p6, turn.

11th and 12th rows K7, turn, p7, turn.
13th and 14th rows K8, turn, p8, turn.
15th and 16th rows K9, turn, p9, turn.
17th row K10, do not turn.

Leave these sts on right-hand needle.

Second, third and fourth base triangles

Work as given for first base triangle. Turn.

★★Left side edge triangle

1st and 2nd rows P2, turn, sl 1, k1, turn.
3rd and 4th rows P into front and back of first st, p2tog, turn, sl 1, k2, turn.
5th and 6th rows P into front and back of first st, p1, p2tog, turn, sl 1, k3, turn.

7th and 8th rows P twice in first st, p2, p2tog, turn, sl 1, k4, turn.

9th and 10th rows P twice in first st, p3, p2tog, turn, sl 1, k5, turn.

11th and 12th rows P twice in first st, p4, p2tog, turn, sl 1, k6, turn.

13th and 14th rows P twice in first st, p5, p2tog, turn, sl 1, k7, turn.

15th and 16th rows P twice in first st, p6, p2tog,

turn, sl 1, k8, turn.

17th row P twice in first st, p7, p2 tog, do not turn (all sts of fourth base triangle have been worked off). Leave these sts on right-hand needle.

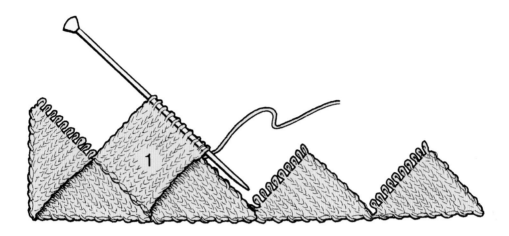

First rectangle

With right-hand needle and wrong side of work facing, pick up and p10 sts along
other edge of fourth base triangle, turn.

1st and 2nd rows Sl 1, k9, turn, p9, p2tog, turn.

Rep 1st and 2nd rows 8 times more.

Next 2 rows Sl 1, k9, turn, p9, p2tog, do not turn (all sts of third base triangle have been worked off). Leave these sts on right-hand needle.

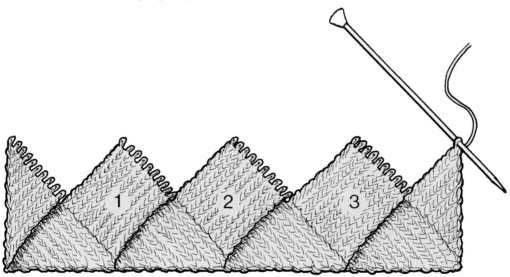

Second and third rectangles

Work as given for first rectangle, noting that the sts will be picked up from third and second base triangles and worked off from second and first base triangles.

Right side edge triangle

With right-hand needle and wrong side facing, pick

up and p10 sts along other side of first base triangle, turn.

1st and 2nd rows K10, turn, p8, p2tog, turn.

3rd and 4th rows K9, turn, p7, p2tog, turn.

5th and 6th rows K8, turn, p6, p2tog, turn.

7th and 8th row K7, turn, p5, p2tog, turn.

9th and 10th rows K6, turn, p4, p2tog, turn.

11th and 12th rows K5, turn, p3, p2tog, turn.
13th and 14th rows K4, turn, p2, p2tog, turn.
15th and 16th rows K3, turn, p1, p2tog, turn.
17th and 18th rows K2, turn, p2tog.
Leave rem st on right-hand needle. Turn. ★★

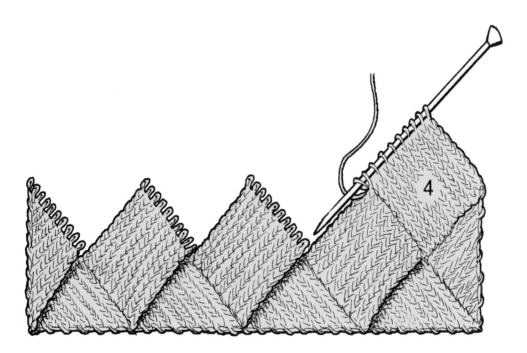

Fourth rectangle.
With right-hand needle and right side of work facing, slip first st, then pick up and k9 sts along inside edge of right side edge triangle, turn. 10 sts.
1st and 2nd rows Sl 1, p9, turn, k9, skpo, turn.
Rep last 2 rows 8 times more.
Next 2 rows Sl 1, p9, turn, k9, skpo, do not turn (all sts of third rectangle have been worked off). Leave these sts on right-hand needle

Fifth rectangle (shown as 3 on second row)
With right-hand needle and right side of work facing, pick up and k10 sts along other side of third rectangle. Work as given for fourth rectangle. (All sts of second rectangle have been worked off).

Sixth and seventh rectangles (shown as 4 and 5 on second row)
Work as given for fifth rectangle, noting that sts will be picked up from second and first rectangles and worked off from first rectangle and left side edge triangle.
Noting that the sts will be worked off and picked up from seventh, sixth, fifth and fourth rectangle instead of base triangles, rep from ★★ to ★★ once more.
Work top edge triangles as follows:

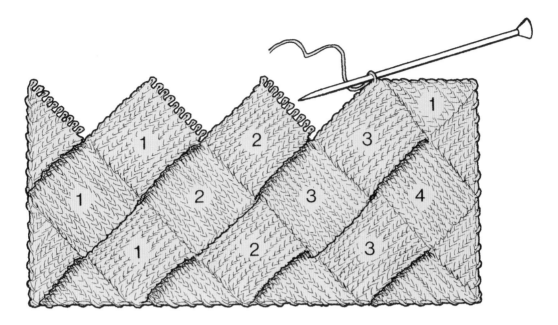

First top triangle

With right-hand needle and right side of work facing, slip first st, then pick up and k 9 sts along inside edge of right side edge triangle, turn. 10 sts.

1st and 2nd rows Sl 1, p9, turn, k9, skpo, turn.

3rd and 4th rows Sl 1, p7, p2tog, turn, k8, skpo, turn.

5th and 6th rows Sl 1, p6, p2tog, turn, k7, skpo, turn.

7th and 8th rows Sl 1, p5, p2tog, turn, k6, skpo, turn.

9th and 10th rows Sl 1, p4, p2tog, turn, k5, skpo, turn.

11th and 12th rows Sl 1, p3, p2tog, turn, k4, skpo, turn.

13th and 14th rows Sl 1, p2, p2tog, turn, k3, skpo, turn.

15th and 16th rows Sl 1, p1, p2tog, turn, k2, skpo, turn.

17th and 18th rows Sl 1, p2tog, turn, k1, skpo, turn.

19th and 20th rows P2tog, turn, skpo, do not turn. Leave rem st on right-hand needle.

Second, third and fourth top triangles

With right-hand needle and right side facing, pick up and k9 sts more along rectangle edge, turn. 10 sts. Complete as given for first top triangle. Fasten off.

Project 14: Two-colour Cushion

This monochromatic cushion cover demonstrates how to work the two-colour entrelac technique.
The back is knitted in two parts in plain stocking stitch with a button opening.

Materials

4 100g hanks of Rowan Magpie in Black (A).
2 100g hanks of Rowan Magpie Tweed in Grey (B).
Pair of 4¹⁄₂mm (No 7/US 7) knitting needles.
6 buttons.
50cm/20in square cushion pad.

Measurements

Approximately 50cm/20in square.

Tension

18 sts and 26 rows to 10cm/4in square over st st on
4¹⁄₂mm (No 7/US 7) needles.

Abbreviations

See page 158.

Front

With 4¹⁄₂ mm (No 7/US 7) needles and A, cast on very
loosely 60 sts.
Work base triangles as follows:
First base triangle
1st and 2nd rows K2, turn, p2, turn.
3rd and 4th rows K3, turn, p3, turn.
5th and 6th rows K4, turn, p4, turn.
7th and 8th rows K5, turn, p5, turn.
9th and 10th rows K6, turn, p6, turn.
11th and 12th rows K7, turn, p7, turn.
13th and 14th rows K8, turn, p8, turn.
15th and 16th rows K9, turn, p9, turn.
17th row K10, do not turn.
Leave these sts on right-hand needle.
Second, third, fourth, fifth and sixth base triangles
Work as given for first base triangle. Break off A and
turn.
★★Left side edge triangle
Join in B.
1st and 2nd rows P2, turn, sl 1, k1, turn.
3rd and 4th rows P twice in first st, p2tog, turn, sl 1,
k2, turn.
5th and 6th rows P twice in first st, p1, p2tog, turn sl 1,
k3, turn.

7th and 8th rows P twice in first st, p2, p2tog, turn, sl 1,
k4, turn.
9th and 10th rows P twice in first st, p3, p2tog, turn, sl
1, k5, turn.
11th and 12th rows P twice in first st, p4, p2tog, turn, sl
1, k6, turn.
13th and 14th rows P twice in first st, p5, p2tog, turn, sl
1, k7, turn.
15th and 16th rows P twice in first st, p6, p2tog, turn, sl
1, k8, turn.
17th row P twice in first st, p7, p2tog, do not turn (all sts
of sixth base triangle have been worked off).
Leave these sts on right-hand needle.
First rectangle
With right-hand needle and wrong side of work facing,
pick up and p10 sts along other edge of sixth base
triangle, turn.
1st and 2nd rows Sl 1, k9, turn, p9, p2tog, turn.
Rep 1st and 2nd rows 8 times more.
Next 2 rows Sl 1, k9, turn, p9, p2tog, do not turn (all sts
of fifth base triangle have been worked off).
Leave these sts on right-hand needle.
Second, third, fourth and fifth rectangles
Work as given for first rectangle, noting that the sts will
be picked up from fifth, fourth, third and second base
triangles and worked off from fourth, third, second and
first base triangles.
Right side edge triangle
With right-hand needle and wrong side facing, pick up
and p10 sts along other side of first base triangle, turn.
1st and 2nd rows K10, turn, p8, p2tog, turn.
3rd and 4th rows K9, turn, p7, p2tog, turn.
5th and 6th rows K8, turn, p6, p2tog, turn.
7th and 8th rows K7, turn, p5, p2tog, turn.
9th and 10th rows K6, turn, p4, p2tog, turn.
11th and 12th rows K5, turn, p3, p2tog, turn.
13th and 14th rows K4, turn, p2, p2tog, turn.
15th and 16th rows K3, turn, p1, p2tog, turn.
17th and 18th rows K2, turn, p2tog and fasten off.
Break off B and turn. **★★★**
Sixth rectangle
Join in A. With right-hand needle and right side of work
facing, pick up and k10 sts along inside edge of right side
edge triangle, turn.
1st and 2nd rows Sl 1, p9, turn, k9, skpo, turn.
Rep last 2 rows 8 times more.
Next 2 rows Sl 1, p9, turn, k9, skpo, do not turn (all sts

of fifth rectangle have been worked off).
Leave these sts on right-hand needle.

Seventh, eight, ninth, tenth and eleventh rectangles
Work as given for sixth rectangle, noting that sts will be picked up from fifth, fourth, third, second and first rectangles and worked off from fourth, third, second, first rectangles and left side edge triangle.★★★★
Noting that the sts will be worked off and picked up from eleventh, tenth, ninth, eight, seventh and sixth rectangle instead of base triangles, rep from ★★ to ★★★★ 4 times, then work from ★★ to ★★★.
Work top edge triangles as follows:

First top triangle
Join in A. With right-hand needle and right side of work facing, pick up and k10 sts along inside edge of right side edge triangle, turn.
1st and 2nd rows Sl 1, p9, turn, k9, skpo, turn.
3rd and 4th rows Sl 1, p7, p2tog, turn, k8, skpo, turn.
5th and 6th rows Sl 1, p6, p2tog, turn, k7, skpo, turn.
7th and 8th rows Sl 1, p5, p2tog, turn, k6, skpo, turn.
9th and 10th rows Sl 1, p4, p2tog, turn, k5, skpo, turn.
11th and 12th rows Sl 1, p3, p2tog, turn, k4, skpo, turn.
13th and 14th rows Sl 1, p2, p2tog, turn, k3, skpo, turn.
15th and 16th rows Sl 1, p1, p2tog, turn, k2, skpo, turn.
17th and 18th rows Sl 1, p2tog, turn, k1, skpo, turn.
19th and 20th rows P2tog, turn, skpo, do not turn.
Leave rem st on right-hand needle.

Second, third, fourth, fifth and sixth top triangles
With right-hand needle and right side facing, pick up and k9 sts more along rectangle edge. 10 sts. Complete as given for first top triangle. Fasten off.

Back

With 4½mm (No 7/US 7) needles and A, cast on 92 sts

for lower part. Work in st st until back measures 40cm/15¾in. Mark each end of last row. Work a further 2cm/¾in in st st. Cast off.
With 4½mm (No 7/US 7) needles and A, cast on 92 sts for upper part. P 1 row.
Buttonhole row K10, [k2 tog, yf, k12] 5 times, k2tog, yf, k10.
Beg with a p row, work in st st until upper part of back measures 11cm/4½in. Cast off.

To Make Up (see also Finishing Workshop)

Place cast on edge of upper part of back in line with markers on lower part of back and secure at side edges. With right sides of back and front together, join all four sides. Turn to right side. Sew buttons on lower back to correspond with buttonholes.

Project 15: Textured Sweater

The entrelac technique is the same as shown before, but by using texture rather than colour you will create a patchwork of cables, bobbles and moss stitch. The sweater has a V-neck with a ribbed collar.

Materials

11 100g balls of Rowan Magpie.
Pair each of 3¾ mm (No 9/US 4) and 4½ mm (No 7/US 7) knitting needles.
Cable needle.

Measurements

To fit bust	81-97	cm
	32-38	in
Actual bust measurement	117	cm
	46	in
Length	68	cm
	26¾	in
Sleeve seam	·46	cm
	18	in

Tension

18 sts and 26 rows to 10cm/4in square over stocking stitch on 4½ mm (No 7/US 7) needles.
19 sts and 30 rows to 10cm/4in square over moss stitch on 3¾ mm (No 9/US 4) needles.

Abbreviations

C4B = sl next 2 sts onto cable needle and leave at back of work, k2, then k2 from cable needle;
C4F = sl next 2 sts onto cable needle and leave at front of work, k2, then k2 from cable needle;
Cr3L = sl next 2 sts onto cable needle and leave at front of work, p1, then k2 from cable needle;
Cr3R = sl next st onto cable needle and leave at back of work, k2, then p1 from cable needle;
mb = k1, p1, k1, p1 all in next st, do not drop the st of left-hand needle but k into the back of it dropping the st, turn, p2tog, p1, p2tog tbl, turn, sl 1, k2tog, psso.
Also see page 158.

Back

With 3¾ mm (No 9/US 4) needles cast on 142 sts.
1st rib row (right side) K2, [p2, k4, p2, k2] to end.
2nd rib row P2, [k2, p4, k2, p2] to end.
3rd and 4th rib rows As 1st and 2nd rows.
5th rib row K2, [p2, C4B, p2, k2] to end.
6th rib row As 2nd row.
Rep 3rd to 6th rows twice more, then work 3rd row again.
Dec row P2, *k2tog, [p2tog] twice, k2tog, p2tog; rep from * to end. 72 sts.
Change to 4½mm (No 7/US 7) needles.
Work base triangles as follows:
First triangle
1st row P1, k1, turn.
2nd row K1, p1, turn.
3rd row P1, k1, p1, turn.
4th row P1, k1, p1, turn.
5th row [P1, k1] twice, turn.
6th row [K1, p1] twice, turn.
Cont in this way, working 1 more st into moss st at end of every right side row, until 18 sts have been worked into moss st. Turn. Moss st 2 more rows on these sts. Do not turn. Leave these sts on right-hand needle.
Second, third and fourth triangles
Work as first triangle. Turn.
★★ Left side edge triangle
1st row K1, p1, turn.
2nd row P1, k1, turn.
3rd row P1 and k1 in first st, p2tog, turn.
4th row P1, k1, p1, turn.
5th row K1 and p1 in first st, k1, p2tog, turn.

6th row [P1, k1] twice, turn.
7th row P1 and k1 in first st, p1, k1, p2tog, turn.
8th row P1, [k1, p1] twice, turn.
Cont in moss st in this way, working twice in first st and last st together with next st of fourth base triangle on every wrong side row until all sts of fourth base triangle have been worked off. 18 sts. Do not turn. Leave these sts on right-hand needle.
Work rectangles as follows:
First rectangle
With wrong side facing, p up 18 sts along other side of fourth base triangle, turn.
1st row With yarn at back of work, sl 1 purlwise, p1, k3, [p1, k1] 4 times, k3, p2, turn.
2nd row K2, p3, [k1, p1] 4 times, p3, k1, skpo, turn.
3rd to 8th rows Rep 1st and 2nd rows 3 times.
9th row With yarn at back of work, sl 1 purlwise, p1, sl next 3 sts onto cable needle and leave at back of work, [p1, k1] twice, then k3 from cable needle, sl next 4 sts onto cable needle and leave at front of work, k3, then [p1, k1] twice from cable needle, p2, turn.
10th row K2, [k1, p1] twice, p6, [k1, p1] twice, k1, skpo, turn.
11th row With yarn at back of work, sl 1 purlwise, p1, [p1, k1] twice, k6, [p1, k1] twice, p2, turn.
12th to 18th rows Rep 10th and 11th rows 3 times, then work 10th row again.
19th row With yarn at back of work, sl 1 purlwise, p1, sl next 4 sts onto cable needle and leave at back of work, k3, then [p1, k1] twice from cable needle, sl next 3 sts onto cable needle and leave at front of work, [p1, k1] twice, then k3 from cable needle, p2, turn.
20th row As 2nd row.
21st to 28th rows Rep 1st and 2nd rows 4 times.
29th to 31st rows Work 9th to 11th rows.
32nd to 36th rows Rep 10th and 11th rows twice, then work 10th row again.
(All sts from third base triangle have been worked off). Do not turn. Leave these sts on right-hand needle.
Second rectangle
With wrong side facing, p up 18 sts along other side of third base triangle, turn.
1st row P1, [k1, p1] twice, k8, p1, [k1, p1] twice, turn.
2nd row [P1, k1] twice, p10, k1, p1, k1, p2tog, turn.
3rd and 4th rows As 1st and 2nd rows.
5th row P1, [k1, p1] twice, C4B, C4F, p1, [k1, p1] twice, turn.
6th to 8th rows Work 2nd to 4th rows.
9th row P1, [k1, p1] twice, C4F, C4B, p1, [k1, p1] twice, turn.
Rep 2nd to 9th rows 3 times, then work 2nd to 4th rows again. (All sts of second base triangle have been worked off). Do not turn. Leave these sts on right-hand needle.

Third rectangle

Picking up sts from other side of second base triangle and working them off first base triangle, work as given for first rectangle.

Right side edge triangle

With wrong side facing, p up 18 sts along other side of first base triangle, turn.

1st row [P1, k1] 9 times, turn.

2nd row [K1, p1] 8 times, k2tog, turn.

3rd row K1, [p1, k1] 8 times, turn.

4th row K1, [p1, k1] 7 times, p2tog, turn.

Cont in moss st in this way, dec 1 st at end of every wrong side row until 2 sts rem. Work 1 row. Turn. Work 2 tog and leave rem st on right-hand needle. Turn.

Fourth rectangle

With right side facing, sl first st onto right hand needle, then k up 17 more sts along inside edge of right side edge triangle, turn. 18 sts.

1st row [P1, k1] 3 times, p2, k5, p1, [k1, p1] twice, turn.

2nd row P1, [k1, p1] twice, p2, mb, p1, Cr3R, p2, k1, p1, k1, p2tog, turn.

3rd row P1, [k1, p1] twice, k2, p2, k4, p1, [k1, p1] twice, turn.

4th row P1, [k1, p1] twice, p3, Cr3R, p3, k1, p1, k1, p2tog, turn.

5th row P1, [k1, p1] twice, k3, p2, k3, p1, [k1, p1] twice, turn.

6th row P1, [k1, p1] twice, p2, Cr3R, p4, k1, p1, k1, p2tog, turn.

7th row P1, [k1, p1] twice, k4, p2, k2, p1, [k1, p1] twice, turn.

8th row P1, [k1, p1] twice, p1, Cr3R, p5, k1, p1, k1, p2tog, turn.

9th row P1, [k1, p1] twice, k5, p2, [k1, p1] 3 times, turn.

10th row P1, [k1, p1] twice, p1, Cr3L, p1, mb, p3, k1, p1, k1, p2tog, turn.

11th row As 7th row.

12th row P1, [k1, p1] twice, p2, Cr3L, p4, k1, p1, k1, p2tog, turn.

13th row As 5th row.

14th row P1, [k1, p1] twice, p3, Cr3L, p3, k1, p1, k1, p2tog, turn.

15th row As 3rd row.

16th row P1, [k1, p1] twice, p4, Cr3L, p2, k1, p1, k1, p2tog, turn.

Rep these 16 rows once more then work 1st to 4th rows again. (All sts of third rectangle have been worked off).

Do not turn. Leave these sts on right-hand needle.

Fifth rectangle

With right side facing, k up 18 sts along other side of third rectangle, turn.

1st row P5, k1, p6, k1, p5, turn.

2nd row K6, p1, C4B, p1, k5, skpo, turn.

3rd row Sl 1, p4, k1, p6, k1, p5, turn.

4th row [K4, p1, k1, p1] twice, k3, skpo, turn.

5th row Sl 1, p2, k1, p1, k1, p6, k1, p1, k1, p3, turn.

6th row K2, [p1, k1] twice, p1, C4B, [p1, k1] 3 times, skpo, turn.

7th row As 5th row.

8th row As 4th row.

9th row As 3rd row.

Rep 2nd to 9th rows 3 times more, then work 2nd to 4th rows again. (All sts of second rectangle have been worked off). Do not turn. Leave these sts on right-hand needle.

Sixth rectangle

With right side facing k up 18 sts along other side of second rectangle, turn. Work as given for fourth rectangle. (All sts of first rectangle have been worked off).

Seventh rectangle

Picking up sts along other side of first rectangle and working them off of left side edge triangle, work as given for fifth rectangle. ★★★

Noting that the sts will be worked off and picked up from seventh, sixth, fifth and fourth rectangles instead of base triangles, work from ★★ to ★★★ 3 times more.

Work top edge triangles as follows:

Left side edge half triangle

Work as left side edge triangle until there are 10 sts on needle thus ending with wrong side row.

Next 2 rows [P1, k1] 4 times, p2tog, turn.

Next row P1, [k1, p1] 3 times, k2tog, turn.

Next row K1, [p1, k1] 3 times, p2tog, turn.

Next 2 rows [P1, k1] 3 times, p2tog, turn.

Next row P1, [k1, p1] twice, k2tog, turn.

Next row K1, [p1, k1] twice, p2tog, turn.

Next 2 rows [P1, k1] twice, p2tog, turn.

Next row P1, k1, p1, k2tog, turn.

Next row K1, k1, p1, p2tog, turn.

Next 2 rows P1, k1, p2tog, turn.

Next row P1, k2tog, turn.

Next row K1, p2tog, pass the second st over first st and fasten off but do not break off the yarn.

First top edge triangle

With wrong side facing, p up 18 sts along edge of rectangle, turn.

1st row [P1, k1] 9 times, turn.

2nd row K1, [p1, k1] 8 times, p2tog, turn.

3rd and 4th rows [P1, k1] 8 times, p2tog, turn.

5th row P1, [k1, p1] 7 times, k2tog, turn.

6th row K1, [p1, k1] 7 times, p2tog, turn.

7th and 8th rows [P1, k1] 7 times, p2tog, turn.

Cont in this way, dec one st at end of every right side

row and working last st tog with next st of rectangle at end of every wrong side row until all sts are worked off and fasten off, but do not break off the yarn.

Second and third top edge triangles
Work as given for first top edge triangle.

Right side edge half triangle
With wrong side facing, p up 18 sts along edge of last rectangle, turn.
Next row [P1, k1] to end.
Next row [K1, p1] to last 2 sts, k2tog.
Next row K1, [p1, k1] to last 2 sts, p2tog.
Cont in moss st in this way, dec one st at end of every row until all sts are decreased. Fasten off.

Front

Work as given for Back to ★★★. Noting that the sts will be worked off and picked up from seventh, sixth, fifth and fourth rectangle instead of base triangles, work from ★★ to ★★★ twice more.

Shape Neck
Work left side edge triangle and the first rectangle for right side of neck, turn.

Right side neck edge triangle
1st row K1, p1, turn.
2nd row P1, k1, turn.
3rd row P1 and k1 in first st, p2 tog, turn.
4th row P1, k1, p1, turn.
5th row K1 and p1 in first st, k1, p2tog, turn.
Cont in moss st in this way, working twice in first st and last st tog with next st of rectangle on every right side row until there are 18 sts. Do not turn. Leave these sts on right-hand needle. Now work seventh rectangle, left side edge half triangle and first top edge triangle. Fasten off. With wrong side facing, slip first 18 sts of rectangle at left side of neck on to a holder. Rejoin yarn and work third rectangle, right side edge triangle and fourth rectangle for left side of neck.

Left side neck edge triangle
With right side facing, k up 18 sts along edge of rectangle, turn.
1st row [K1, p1] 9 times, turn.
2nd row [P1, k1] 8 times, p2tog, turn.
3rd row P1, [k1, p1] 8 times.
4th row P1, [k1, p1] 7 times, k2tog.
Cont in moss st in this way, dec one st at end of every right side row until all sts are worked off. Fasten off but do not break off the yarn. Work third top edge triangle and right side edge half triangle.

Sleeves

With 3¾ mm (No 9/US 4) needles cast on 56 sts.
1st rib row (right side) P2, k2, [p2, k4, p2, k2] to last 2 sts, p2.

2nd rib row K2, p2, [k2, p4, k2, p2] to last 2 sts, k2.
3rd and 4th rib rows As 1st and 2nd rows.
5th rib row P2, k2, [p2, C4B, p2, k2] to last 2 sts, p2.
6th row As 2nd row.
Rep 3rd to 6th rows twice more, then work 3rd and 4th rows again.
Change to 4½mm (No 7/US 7) needles.
1st row [K1, p1] 12 times, k8, [p1, k1] 12 times.
2nd row [K1, p1] 12 times, p8, [p1, k1] 12 times.
3rd row [K1, p1] 12 times, C4B, C4F, [p1, k1] 12 times.
4th row As 2nd row.
5th and 6th rows As 1st and 2nd rows.
7th row [K1, p1] 12 times, C4F, C4B, [p1, k1] 12 times.
8th row As 2nd row.
These 8 rows form patt. Cont in patt, inc one st at each end of next row and 5 foll 4th rows then on every foll 6th row until there are 94 sts on needle, working inc sts into moss st patt. Work straight until sleeve measures 46cm/18in from beg, ending with a wrong side row. Cast off in patt.

Neckband

Place markers at neck edge three quarters way down from top edge on each side neck edge triangle. With 3¾mm (No 9/US 4) needles, right side facing and beginning at marker, k up 7 sts down left front neck then k 18 sts of rectangle, k up 25 sts up right front neck to marker. 50 sts.
1st rib row P2, [k2, p2] to end.
2nd rib row K2, [p2, k2] 5 times, p1, k2tog, skpo, p1, [k2, p2] 5 times, k2.
3rd rib row Rib 22, p2tog tbl, p2tog, rib to end.
4th rib row Rib 21, k2tog, skpo, rib to end.
Rib 3 more rows, dec at centre as before. Cast off in rib, dec at centre as before.

Collar

Join shoulder seams.
With 3¾mm (No 9/US 4) needles, right side facing and beginning at marker, k up 24 sts up right front neck, 34 sts across back neck and 24 sts down left front neck to marker. 82 sts.
Inc row K2, [k twice in next, k1] to end. 122 sts.
Beg with 2nd row, work 7 rows in rib as given for back welt.
Change to 4½mm (No 7/US 7) needles and work a further 14 rows in patt. Cast off in patt.

To Make Up (see also Finishing Workshop)

Join row ends of neckband to collar. Sew on sleeves, placing centre of sleeves to shoulder seams. Join side and sleeve seams.

CHAPTER SEVEN

Decorative Details Workshop

MANY DESIGNS CAN be enhanced by the addition of embellishments such as embroidery, knitting with sequins and beads, or finishing with a decorative hem. For example, a diamond-patterned jacket can be given a folkloric or Tyrolean look by embroidering flowers within the stitch pattern and a lace edging or a picot hem can be a pretty alternative to the usual ribbed welt. Swiss darning can be used to work small areas of colour rather than knitting them in and sometimes in my designs I have used it to create a raised, more prominent effect. It can also be invaluable in masking errors in colour patterning.

Making fringes, pompons and cords is a great way to introduce children to yarns and working with their hands in a way that they can easily grasp. After some frustrating attempts to teach a group of seven year olds in my son's school I had a breakthrough in my final class when we made pompon chicks and snowmen, with the result that I did not feel quite such a failure and they had something to show for their efforts.

Embroidery Stitches

Embroidery can be a really effective way of enhancing a plain garment. Decorative stitches can be placed within a cable, on a border or collar or used to liven up a pocket. Remember that it is much easier to embroider the garment pieces before they are sewn up.

Stem Stitch

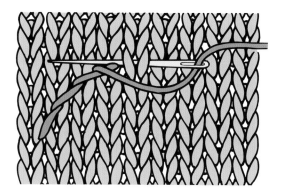

This is a continuous line of stitches, worked from left to right in a similar way to backstitch (see page 152), but each stitch overlaps the previous one by half its length (as on the wrong side of backstitch).

Cross Stitch

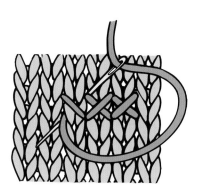

Cross stitches are created by two stitches crossing each other at right angles. They can be worked across one or two stitches and rows as required, inserting the needle between the stitches to avoid splitting the yarn.

Chain Stitch

This can be worked vertically, horizontally or diagonally across the fabric or in a curve. Insert the needle in the same place from which it has emerged and bring it out for the next stitch, looping the thread over the tip of the needle.

Lazy Daisy Stitch

This is a method of working individual chain stitches, which are fastened with a small tying stitch, to form 'petals' which can be grouped together to make a 'flower' of 4, 5 or more petals.

Swiss Darning Horizontally

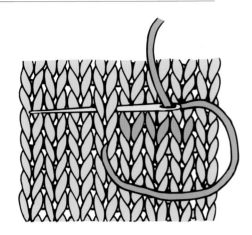

Work from right to left. Thread a tapestry needle with the same weight of yarn and weave in the yarn invisibly at the back of the work. Bring the needle out at the base of the first stitch to be covered, take it around the top of the stitch, then insert the needle back through the base of the same stitch, thus covering the original stitch completely. For the next stitch bring the needle through at the base of the next stitch to the left. Continue in this way until the appropriate stitches have been covered.

Blanket Stitch

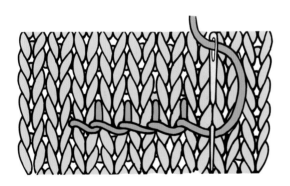

This stitch may be used along an edge where there is no ribbing, for example around a neck edge or for decorative purposes. It is a series of evenly spaced straight vertical stitches, looped at the end where the needle emerges, worked from left to right.

Swiss Darning Vertically

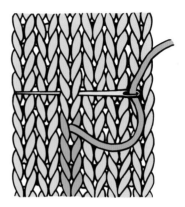

Work from bottom to top. Bring the needle out at the base of the first stitch to be covered, then take it around the top of the stitch. Insert the needle back through the base of the same stitch, then bring it up through the base of the stitch above, thus forming a vertical chain.

French Knot

This is often worked in the centre of a flower of lazy daisy stitches. Bring the needle from the back to the front of the work and wind the yarn twice around the needle, pulling it gently to tighten the twists. Take the needle back through the same place and draw the yarn through, thus forming a small knot on the right side. If the knot tends to slip through to the wrong side, insert the needle half a stitch further on to avoid this.

Loop Knitting

Although loop knitting can be used to work an all-over fabric for a garment, it is probably used to best effect in creating a mock fur fabric for collars and cuffs.

Making A Single Loop

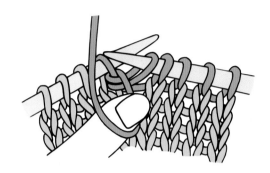

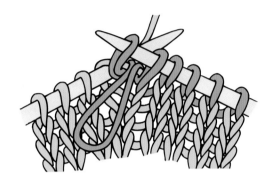

1 On the right side of the work, knit to the position of the loop. Knit the next stitch, but do not allow the loop to drop off the left-hand needle. Bring the yarn to the front between the needles and wind it once clockwise around your left thumb.

2 Take the yarn to the back again between the needles and knit into the same stitch on the left-hand needle – so making two stitches out of the original one. Slip the stitch off the left-hand needle.

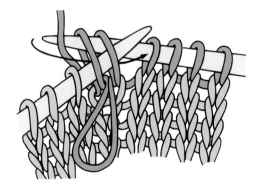

3 Place both stitches back on the left-hand needle and knit them together through the back of the loops to complete the loop stitch.

TIPS: LOOP KNITTING

Either of these loop knitting techniques can be used to create a mock fur fabric: the cluster technique will produce a thicker, denser 'fur' than the single loop technique. However, do bear in mind that while the loops formed by the single loop technique can be cut without the fabric unravelling, the cluster loops cannot be cut as the loops themselves form part of the stitch.
Loops can also be used to form a fringed edge on a scarf or sweater as an alternative to the traditional method of fringing shown opposite.
Loop knitting should not be used on garments for a baby or a small child as they can easily catch their fingers in the loops.

Making A Cluster Of Loops

1 On a wrong side row, work to the position of the loop. Take yarn to the back (right side) of the work and insert right-hand needle knitwise into next stitch. Depending on the size of loop, put one or two fingers of your left hand behind the right-hand needle and wind yarn three times around the point of the right-hand needle and your fingers in clockwise direction, ending with yarn on needle.

2 Use the right-hand needle to draw the loops though the stitch without allowing the original stitch to drop off the left-hand needle.

3 Remove your fingers from the loops, replace the new loops on the right-hand needle back on the left-hand needle and knit them together with the original stitch through the back of the stitches. Holding the loops down at the back of the work with the fingers of your left hand, pull the loops firmly through to the right side.

Fringing

This is the traditional way to trim a scarf but it is not suitable for babies as the strands can come loose.

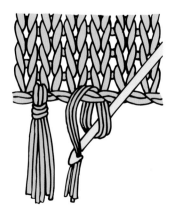

The number of strands in each tassel decides the thickness of the fringe, as well as the distance between each tassel.

Cut the required number of lengths for one tassel slightly more than twice the length of the finished tassel. Fold the strands in half and draw the folded end through the edge of the knitted fabric using a crochet hook. Draw the loose ends of yarn through the loop, and draw up firmly to form a knot. Trim the ends to neaten once the fringe is complete.

Knitting With Beads

Perfect for a lightly sprinkled surface, these beads 'hang' very slightly on the surface of the fabric from the strand at the front of the slipped stitch.

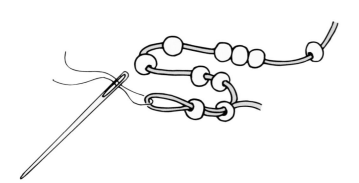

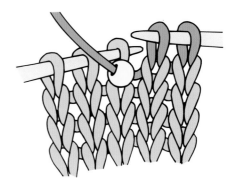

1 Fold a length of sewing cotton in half and thread both ends through a sewing needle. Thread the end of the yarn through the loop in the sewing cotton and fold it back on itself. Thread beads along the needle, down the sewing cotton and onto the yarn until you have the number of beads on the yarn that your pattern requires.

2 On a right side row, knit to the position of the beaded stitch. Bring the yarn forward to the front of the work and push a bead down the yarn close to the last stitch so that it lies over the front of the next stitch.

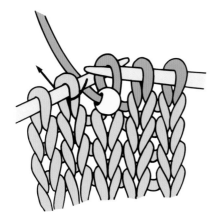

3 Slip the next stitch purlwise, leaving the bead in front of the slipped stitch. Take the yarn to the back and continue the work as normal.

TIPS: BEADS

Most patterns specify the number of beads to be threaded on to each ball of yarn. If not, thread up one ball with more beads than you will need, then count the number used after completing that ball. It is important to thread on the correct number of beads (or more) before beginning to knit; once the ball is started you will not be able to add more unless you unwind the ball and add them from the other end, or break the yarn. Beads should be a suitable weight for the yarn and must have a large enough hole for double-thickness yarn to pass through. Beads can be knitted at random or in an evenly spaced design or they can be incorporated into a lace or texture pattern. The fabric should be fairly firm or the beads may slip through to the wrong side and the additional weight of the beads may drag a loosely knitted garment out of shape.

Picot Hem

This is delicate edging that is particularly attractive on babywear. When the hem is folded back the row of eyelet holes creates small picot points on the edge of the garment.

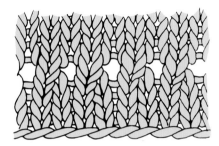

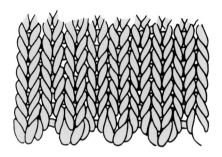

Cast on an odd number of stitches using needles two sizes smaller than those used for the main fabric and work in stocking stitch for the required depth, ending with a purl row. (This hem can be very narrow – perhaps only 2 rows before the eyelets.)

Work the eyelet hole row as follows: knit the first stitch, *bring the yarn forward to the front of the work between the needles then knit the next two stitches together; repeat from * to the end of the row.

Continue in stocking stitch and the larger needle size for the rest of the edging, although the main fabric could be worked in another stitch.

The hem is folded back along the eyelet hole row and sewn in place to form an undulating edge with picot points.

Double Crochet Edging

This can be used as a decorative border or to neaten edges without welts. Work it in the same weight yarn as the main fabric with a crochet hook the same size or slightly larger than the needles used.

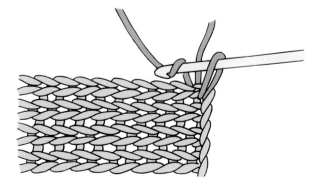

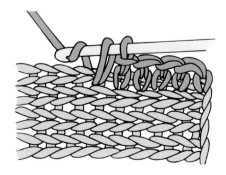

1 Insert the hook under the first stitch at the right-hand end from front to back, wind the yarn around the hook and draw a loop through from the back. Wind the yarn around the hook again and draw it through the loop on the hook.

2 Insert the hook one or two rows or stitches along, draw a loop through then wind the yarn around the hook and draw it through the two loops on the hook. Check that the edging is not so loose that it flutes, or so tight that it distorts the fabric.

Making A Pompon

Pompons are often used to decorate hats or make soft toys. Children find them fun to make and love choosing colours and thicknesses from your yarn oddments box.

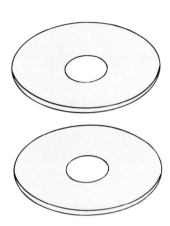

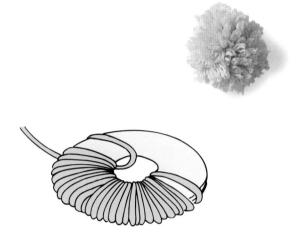

1 Decide on the size of the pompon required, then cut two circles of card, the diameter of which should be slightly bigger than the size of the finished pompon. Cut a smaller hole in the centre of each circle, about half the size of the original diameter. The larger the hole is the fuller the pompon will be, but if you make it too large the pompon will be oval shaped instead of round.

2 Holding the two circles together, wind the yarn around the ring (using several strands at a time for speed), until the ring is completely covered. As the hole in the centre gets smaller, you may find it easier to use a sewing needle to pass the yarn through.

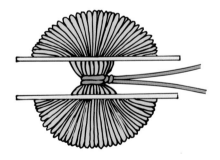

3 Cut all around the yarn at the outside edge, between the two rings, using a pair of sharp scissors, Make sure all the yarn has been cut.

4 Separate the circles slightly, and tie a length of yarn into a firm knot between them, leaving enough to sew the pompon in place. Remove the two circles and fluff out the pompon. Trim the ends of the yarn to produce a smooth edge.

Making A Twisted Cord

Twisted cords can be used to thread through eyelet holes to draw the fabric in or to use as decoration. They can be made to any size or thickness.

1 Cut the required number of strands of yarn 2 to 3 times the length of the finished cord. For example, 4 strands of yarn 100cm/40in long will produce cord 8 strands thick and approximately 40cm/16in long. Knot the strands together at each end, making sure they are of equal length.

2 Attach one end to a hook or door handle, and insert a knitting needle through the other. Turn the knitting needle clockwise until the strands are tightly twisted. The tighter the yarns are twisted, the firmer the finished cord will be, but this will also reduce the finished length.

3 Holding the cord in the centre with one hand, bring both ends of the cord together, allowing the two halves to twist together. Keep the cord fairly straight to avoid tangling and smooth it out evenly. Knot the cut ends together and trim. Decide on the length of the cord, tie a knot in the folded end at the required point and cut the ends.

TIPS: CORDS AND PLAITS
You can twist two or three different coloured yarns together to produce a striped cord. This style of trim is traditionally used to edge cushions.

Another easy and popular type of trimming is a plaited cord (below). This is made in exactly the same way as hair is plaited. You will need several strands of yarn for each 'branch' of the plait, each strand 25% longer than the finished plait will be. Again, try plaiting different colours together.

Decorative Details Stitch Library

Interesting detailing can be used to enhance a plain design or to introduce a fresh look to a classic. I often use a lace edging as a trim for a collar and cuffs or as an alternative to ribbed welts as it can add delicacy to a cotton cabled cardigan. Most of the lace edgings shown here are worked lengthwise over a relatively small number of stitches and are sewn on to the garment with mattress stitch (see page 150).

Diamond Edging

Worked lengthwise over 12 sts.
Note: due to the nature of the pattern the number of sts varies on some rows.
1st and every alt row (right side) K1, yrn, p2tog, k to end
2nd row K2, yf, k3, yf, skpo, k2, yrn, p2tog, k1. 13 sts.
4th row K2, yf, k5, yf, skpo, k1, yrn, p2tog, k1. 14 sts.
6th row K2, yf, k7, yf, skpo, yrn, p2tog, k1. 15 sts.
8th row K1, k2tog, yf, skpo, k3, k2tog, yf, k2, yrn, p2tog, k1. 14 sts.
10th row K1, k2tog, yf, skpo, k1, k2tog, yf, k3, yrn, p2tog, k1. 13 sts.
12th row K1, k2tog, yf, sl 1, k2tog, psso, yf, k4, yrn, p2tog, k1. 12 sts.
Rep these 12 rows.

Double Diamond Edging

Worked lengthwise over 9 sts.
Note: due to the nature of the pattern the number of sts varies on some rows.
1st and every alt row (right side) Knit to end.
2nd row K3, [k2tog, yf] twice, k1, yf, k1. 10 sts.
4th row K2, [k2tog, yf] twice, k3, yf, k1. 11 sts.
6th row K1, [k2tog, yf] twice, k5, yf, k1. 12 sts.
8th row K3, [yf, k2tog] twice, k1, k2tog, yf, k2tog. 11 sts.
10th row K4, yf, k2tog, yf, k3tog, yf, k2tog. 10 sts.
12th row K5, yf, k3tog, yf, k2tog. 9 sts.
Rep these 12 rows.

Leaf Edging

Worked lengthwise over 8 sts.
Note: due to the nature of the pattern the number of sts varies on some rows.
1st row (right side) K5, yf, k1, yf, k2. 10sts.
2nd row P6, inc in next st by knitting into front

and back of it, k3. 11 sts.

3rd row K4, p1, k2, yf, k1, yf, k3. 13 sts.

4th row P8, inc in next st, k4. 14 sts.

5th row K4, p2, k3, yf, k1, yf, k4. 16 sts.

6th row P10, inc in next st, k5. 17 sts.

7th row K4, p3, k4, yf, k1, yf, k5. 19 sts.

8th row P12, inc in next st, k6. 20 sts.

9th row K4, p4, yb, skpo, k7, k2tog, k1. 18 sts.

10th row P10, inc in next st, k7. 19 sts.

11th row K4, p5, yb, skpo, k5, k2tog, k1. 17 sts.

12th row P8, inc in next st, k2, p1, k5. 18 sts.

13th row K4, p1, k1, p4, yb, skpo, k3, k2tog, k1. 16 sts.

14th row P6, inc in next st, k3, p1, k5. 17 sts.

15th row K4, p1, k1, p5, yb, skpo, k1, k2tog, k1. 15 sts.

16th row P4, inc in next st, k4, p1, k5. 16 sts.

17th row K4, p1, k1, p6, yb, sl 1, k2tog, psso, k1. 14 sts.

18th row P2tog, counting the p st on right-hand needle as first st cast off 5 sts (1 st on right-hand needle), k1, p1, k5. 8 sts.

Rep these 18 rows.

Garter Stitch Edging

Worked lengthwise over 10 sts.

Note: due to the nature of the pattern the number of sts varies on some rows.

1st row (right side) K3, [yf, k2tog] twice, yf and around needle to make 2 sts, k2tog, k1. 11 sts.

2nd row K3, p1, k2, [yf, k2tog] twice, k1.

3rd row K3, [yf, k2tog] twice, k1, yf and around needle, k2tog, k1. 12 sts.

4th row K3, p1, k3, [yf, k2tog] twice, k1.

5th row K3, [yf, k2tog] twice, k2, yf and around needle, k2tog, k1. 13 sts.

6th row K3, p1, k4, [yf, k2tog] twice, k1.

7th row K3, [yf, k2tog] twice, k6.

8th row Cast off 3 sts (1 st on right-hand needle), k4, [yf, k2tog] twice, k1. Rep these 8 rows.

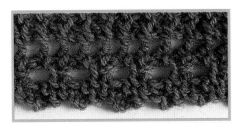

Bird's Eye Edging

Worked lengthwise over 7 sts.

Note: the number of sts varies on rows.

1st row (right side) K1, [k2tog, yf and yarn round needle to make 2 sts] twice, k2. 9sts.

2nd row K3, [p1, k2] twice.

3rd row K1, k2tog, yf and around needle, k2tog, k4.

4th row Cast off 2 sts (1 st on right-hand needle), k3, p1, k2. 7 sts.

Rep these 4 rows.

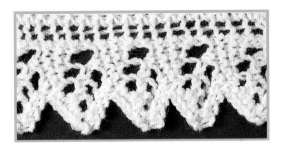

Willow Edging

Worked lengthwise over 10 sts.

Note: due to the nature of the pattern the number of sts varies on some rows.

1st row (right side) Sl 1, k2, yf, k2tog, [yf and around needle to make 2 sts, k2tog] twice, k1. 12 sts.

2nd row K3, [p1, k2] twice, yf, k2tog, k1.

3rd row Sl 1, k2, yf, k2tog, k2, [yf and around needle, k2tog] twice, k1. 14 sts.

4th row K3, p1, k2, p1, k4, yf, k2tog, k1.

5th row Sl 1, k2, yf, k2tog, k4, [yf and around needle, k2tog] twice, k1. 16 sts.

6th row K3, p1, k2, p1, k6, yf, k2tog, k1.

7th row Sl 1, k2, yf, k2tog, k11.

8th row Cast off 6 sts, (1 st on right-hand needle), k6, yf, k2tog, k1. 10 sts.

Rep these 8 rows.

Moss And Faggot

Worked lengthwise over 17 sts.

Note: due to the nature of the pattern the number of sts varies on some rows.

1st row (right side) K2, yf, k3, yf, k2tog, [p1, k1] 5 times. 18 sts.

2nd row Yon (to make 1 st), k2tog, [k1, p1] 3 times, k1, k2tog, yf, k5, yf, k2. 19 sts.

3rd row K2, yf, k1, k2tog, yf, k1, yf, k2tog, k1, yf, k2tog, [p1, k1] 4 times. 20 sts.

4th row Yon, k2tog, [k1, p1] twice, [k1, k2tog, yf] twice, k3, yf, k2tog, k1, yf, k2. 21 sts.

5th row K2, yf, k1, k2tog, yf, k5, yf, k2tog, k1, yf, k2tog, [p1, k1] 3 times. 22 sts.

6th row Yon, k2tog, k1, p1, [k1, k2tog, yf] twice, k7, yf, k2tog, k1, yf, k2. 23 sts.

7th row [K2tog, k1, yf] twice, k2tog, k3, [k2tog, yf, k1] twice, [p1, k1] 3 times. 22 sts.

8th row Yon, k2tog, [k1, p1] 3 times, yon, k2tog, k1, yf, k2tog, [k1, k2tog, yf] twice, k1, k2tog. 21 sts.

9th row [K2tog, k1, yf] twice, k3tog, yf, k1, k2tog, yf, [k1, p1] 4 times, k1. 20 sts.

10th row Yon, k2tog, [k1, p1] 4 times, yon, k2tog, k3, k2tog, yf, k1, k2tog. 19 sts.

11th row K2tog, k1, yf, k2tog, k1, k2tog, yf, [k1, p1] 5 times, k1. 18 sts.

12th row Yon, k2tog, [k1, p1] 5 times, yon, k3tog, yf, k1, k2tog. 17 sts.

Rep these 12 rows.

Wavy Border

Worked lengthwise over 15 sts.

Note: due to the nature of the pattern the number of sts varies on some rows.

1st and every alt row (wrong side) K2, purl to last 2 sts, k2.

2nd row Sl 1, k4, sl 1, k2tog, psso, k2, [yf, k2tog] twice, k1. 13 sts.

4th row Sl 1, k3, skpo, k2, [yf, k2tog] twice, k1. 12 sts.

6th row Sl 1, k2, skpo, k2, [yf, k2tog] twice, k1. 11 sts.

8th row Sl 1, k1, skpo, k2, [yf, k2tog] twice, k1. 10 sts.

10th row K1, skpo, k2, yf, k1, yf, k2tog, yf, k2. 11 sts.

12th row Sl 1, [k3, yf] twice, k2tog, yf, k2. 13 sts.

14th row Sl 1, k3, yf, k5, yf, k2tog, yf, k2. 15 sts.

Rep these 14 rows.

Scallop Edging

Begins with multiple of 13 sts + 2 sts. The number of sts to a repeat varies on some rows.

1st row (right side) K3, ★skpo, work 5tog thus: sl 2, k3tog, pass 2 slipped sts over, k2tog, k4; rep from ★ to last 12 sts, skpo, work 5tog, k2tog, k3.

2nd row P4, ★yrn, p1, yrn, p6; rep from ★ to last 5 sts, yrn, p1, yrn, p4.

3rd row K1, yf, ★k2, skpo, k1, k2tog, k2, yf; rep

from ★ to last st, k1.

4th row P2, ★yrn, p2, yrn, p3, yrn, p2, yrn, p1; rep from ★ to last st, p1.

5th row K2, yf, k1, ★yf, skpo, k1, sl 1, k2tog, psso, k1, k2tog, [yf, k1] 3 times; rep from ★ to last 12 sts, yf, skpo, k1, sl 1, k2tog, psso, k1, k2tog, yf, k1, yf, k2.

6th row Purl to end.

7th row K5, ★yf, work 5tog, yf, k7; rep from ★ to last 10 sts, yf, work 5tog, yf, k5.

8th to 10th rows Knit to end.

Fan Edging

Worked lengthwise over 14 sts.

Note: Due to the nature of the pattern the number of sts varies on some rows.

1st row (wrong side) K2, yf, k2tog, k5, yf, k2tog, yf, k3. 15 sts.

2nd and every alt row K1, yf, k2tog, k to end.

3rd row K2, yf, k2tog, k4, [yf, k2tog] twice, yf, k3. 16 sts.

5th row K2, yf, k2tog, k3, [yf, k2tog] 3 times, yf, k3. 17 sts.

7th row K2 yf, k2tog, k2, [yf, k2tog] 4 times, yf, k3. 18 sts.

9th row K2, yf, k2tog, k1, [yf, k2tog] 5 times, yf, k3. 19 sts.

11th row K2, yf, k2tog, k1, k2tog, [yf, k2tog] 5 times, k2. 18 sts.

13th row K2, yf, k2tog, k2, k2tog, [yf, k2tog] 4 times, k2. 17 sts.

15th row K2, yf, k2tog, k3, k2tog, [yf, k2tog] 3 times, k2. 16 sts.

17th row K2, yf, k2tog, k4, k2tog, [yf, k2tog] twice, k2. 15 sts.

19th row K2, yf, k2tog, k5, k2tog, yf, k2tog, k2. 14 sts.

20th row K1, yf, k2tog, k to end.

Rep these 20 rows.

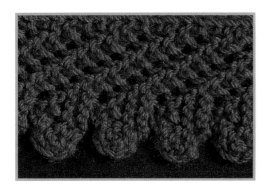

Diagonal Rib And Scallop

Worked lengthwise over 8 sts.

Note: due to the nature of the pattern the number of sts varies on some rows.

1st Foundation row (right side) K6, k into front and back of next st, yf, sl 1 purlwise. 9 sts.

2nd Foundation row K1 tbl, k2, yf, skpo, k1 skpo, yf, sl 1 purlwise. 9 sts.

1st row K1 tbl, k7, k into front and back of last st, turn and cast on 2 sts. 12 sts.

2nd row K1, k into front and back of next st, k2, [yf, skpo, k1] twice, yf, k1, yf, sl 1 purlwise. 14 sts.

3rd row K1 tbl, k11, k into front and back of next st, yf, sl 1 purlwise. 15 sts.

4th row K1 tbl, k into front and back of next st, k2 [yf, skpo, k1] 3 times, k1, yf, sl 1 purlwise. 16 sts.

5th row K1tbl, k13, k2tog. 15 sts.

6th row Sl 1 purlwise, k1, psso, skpo, k4, [yf, skpo, k1] twice, yf, sl 1 purlwise. 13 sts.

7th row K1 tbl, k10, k2tog. 12 sts.

8th row Cast off 3 sts (1 st on right-hand needle) k2, yf, skpo, k1, yf, skpo, yf, sl 1 purlwise. 9 sts.

Rep these 8 rows.

CHAPTER EIGHT

Design Workshop

NOW YOU ARE ready to create your own design. Along the way you have learned all the techniques and skills that are required, a knowledge of yarns and how they behave, tension, shaping, and how to work in texture and colour. All that is required now is confidence and a knowledge of simple arithmetic. In the first instance I hope to demystify the process of compiling a pattern and any problems with the latter can be easily solved with a calculator!

You may already know by now whether you have a preference for stitch texture or colour, or perhaps you love the idea of combining the two. You may find, like me, that the sketching and doodling stage sets your creative mind free and the ideas tumble out, only to be brought up short when those same ideas don't translate as well on the needles.

Be patient, sometimes you may have to work five or six sample swatches before you hit upon the one that you know is right. Keep trying and you will get there in the end.

In this workshop you will be shown how to compile a very basic pattern for a child's sweater. This will give you the grounding to enable you to go on and experiment with more challenging shapes and styles.

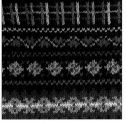

Designing Handknits

Designing and making your own handknits can be both exciting and rewarding and in this workshop I want to show you how you can use the practical techniques you have learned previously as a basis for creating your own design.

Before You Start

After the initial stages of experimenting by knitting up swatches in different yarns, stitches and shades, there are some points to remember before you start to compile your first pattern which will help you achieve a successful finished garment.

Choosing A Style

It is best to begin with simple sweater styles, preferably with dropped shoulders and as little shaping as possible, like the one I have sketched on this page. This will allow you to concentrate on the fabric and the style without worrying about any complicated arithmetic or the effect that increases and decreases will have on a pattern repeat.

Choosing A Yarn

Suit your design to the yarn you want to use and *vice versa*: a textured stitch will not show up as well in a mohair, chenille or brushed yarn and what looks stunning in a cotton yarn may not look as effective in wool.

Some ribbon yarns will drop or become unstable when used for longline garments such as tunics, and some yarns may only be really suitable for use in edgings and decorative trims.

If you are using a heavier weight yarn, or a stitch pattern that creates a fairly firm fabric, it is important that the proportions of your garment are fairly generous, particularly the underarm measurement, to give ease of movement. Remember that the purpose of the intricate stitches and cables on the original Aran sweaters was to create a weatherproof garment, but a solid fabric can be uncomfortable to wear if it fits the body too closely.

Designing For Children

If you are designing for children avoid using yarns that feel harsh or may irritate their skin, especially if there is a high neckline.

Babies usually dislike having garments pulled over their heads and it can be a struggle to dress them if a neck is a little too tight, particularly when a baby is too small to sit up on its own.

To prevent your distress as well as theirs, sweaters knitted for babies should have wide neck openings with button fastenings on one or both shoulders, or an envelope neck which is wide enough to pass easily over their heads. Involve the child in the design of their garment, it is a wonderful way to let them participate in your project, and all to often the child can be the last person to be consulted when a design is being knitted up for them.

Design And Detail

To me, the most important part of any design is to achieve harmony within all parts of it.
On this page are some of the elements you should consider when designing a garment.

Designing With Patterns

Life, of course, is always a lot simpler when you are designing in stocking stitch. If you are using a stitch or colour pattern with a repeat, you will need to accommodate that repeat into the proportions and this may make the garment smaller or larger than you would have liked.

It is important to see the garment as a whole. For instance, does the depth of the neck interrupt a pattern in an unattractive way? If you are working with bands of Fair Isle it is better to start your neck between the bands so the colour pattern isn't distorted by the neckband when it is picked up later. You may need to use a dropped shoulder style because a set-in sleeve will also cut into a pattern. The art of design is sometimes the art of compromise.

Designing With Motifs

If I am creating a design that has individual motifs worked over the garment, I will chart out the area I have to work within on graph paper by graphing out the number of stitches and rows and the space for the neckband. I will then graph out each individual motif, cut fairly closely them and then arrange them within the graph of my garment. I will move them around and adjust them until they satisfy all my requirements – does the space between motifs look right? Too much space between some and too little between others can make the design look unbalanced.

Designing Aran Styles

If I am working on an Aran with different pattern panels I will knit the panels seperately and switch them around until I find the sequence I feel works best. I may change a 4-stitch cable to a 6-stitch cable because I feel the latter provides a stronger look. I will try to find cables that have a common link – it may be that they use moss stitch or garter stitch which can also be used as a selvedge stitch.

Designing Edgings

I feel that welts or edgings are as important as the main part of the garment; you wouldn't put a beautiful picture in an ugly frame, particularly if you were the artist! Of course, sometimes simple ribbed edgings are perfect, but normally we can do better. On an Aran style, for instance run the small cables and bobbles down into the rib, and on a colour design, rather than work the welts just in the main colour, a single stripe or edging in the contrast shades can pull all the colour work together. There is also a wide variety of edgings (see the Decorative Details Stitch Library, pages 136–139) that can be used.

Getting It Right

Remember, when you are beginning to design, do not be afraid of making mistakes. There are very few wrongs and rights, your goal is to feel the excitement and satisfaction of creating something that is special to you.

Designing A Simple Sweater

To begin with I will take you through the stages of creating a very basic sweater to fit a child.
The sweater is worked in stocking stitch and has dropped shoulders and a round neck.

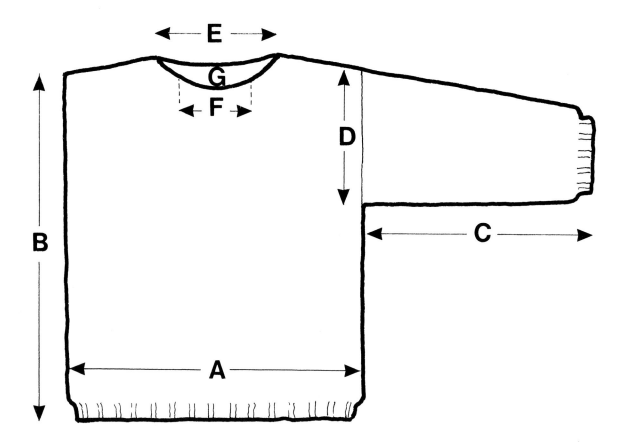

When calculating a pattern the best method by far is to take the overall measurements of a garment of which you already like the proportions. However, for the sake of this exercise I have based the proportions on the following simple formula which will guide you through compiling your first basic pattern (see also pages 146-147).

Draw a diagram of a round-necked sweater with the following measurements marked as above: width of back and front A, length to shoulder B, sleeve length C, armhole depth D, back neck width E, front neck width F, neck depth G.

Work a tension square (see page 13) with the yarn of your choice and the appropriate needles. Measure the number of stitches and rows to 10cm/4in and then calculate the number of stitches and rows to 1cm/1in.

Back

Multiply this figure by the measurement of the width of the back (A) and this will give you the number of stitches to cast on.

For instance in the pattern example I will be showing you I have used Rowan Handknit Cotton which has a tension of 20 sts and 28 rows to 10cm/4in, or 2 sts and 2.8 rows to 1cm/5 sts and 7 rows to 1in. Therefore, to achieve a back measurement of 38 cm/15in you would cast on 38 sts x 2/15 sts x 5, which is 76 sts/75 sts, plus 2 extra stitches to allow for your seam when you are sewing up the finished sweater.

This seam allowance is important as with a chunkier yarn the stitches that you take up in your seam can make a difference to your overall width.

Single rib is the most commonly used border stitch and is usually knitted on needles which are two sizes smaller than those used on the main fabric. The length of the rib is taken away from the overall length and the figure you are left with is multiplied by the number of rows to 1cm/1in to give the total amount of rows to be worked after the rib.

The number of stitches allowed for each shoulder is calculated by subtracting the back neck stitches from the total and then dividing the number by two.

Front

The front is worked the same way as given for the back until it is approximately 6cm/3in shorter than the back. Because one side of the neck is worked first, half the front neck (F) stitches should be subtracted from half the front stitches to give you the number of stitches required for the first side of the neck. By subtracting the shoulder stitches from this amount you will know how many stitches you need to decrease for the neck shaping.

Multiply the neck depth (G) by the row tension and this will give you the number of rows to be worked. Calculate the frequency of decreases. For a round neck, as in this design, you will need to have a few straight rows at the top of each side of the neck. So, divide the number of rows by the number of stitches to be decreased, allowing for a few straight rows at the top, and then decrease on every row or alternate row as the number of rows allows.

For example, if you have 20 rows and 7 stitches to decrease, divide 14 (20 rows minus 6 straight rows) by 7 which equals 2, so you would decrease on every alternate row.

Graph paper can be very helpful when working out these shapings.

Sleeves

On a dropped shoulder sweater there is no armhole shaping and the sleeves are shorter than those of a sweater with a set-in sleeve. This is because the dropped shoulders are wider and the extra width as it 'drops' over the shoulder adds to the sleeve length.

Decide on the width of the sleeve at the lower edge and calculate the number of stitches you require. Ribbed cuffs are usually fairly narrow to fit snugly to the wrist. Therefore less stitches are cast on but they are then increased on the last row of rib to the number of stitches required for the lower sleeve.

The width of the top of the sleeve is wider than the bottom. (Half the top of the sleeve is the armhole depth D.) By subtracting the number of stitches at the bottom of the sleeve from those at the top you will know how many stitches are needed to be increased along the length of the sleeve, omitting the cuff.

As increases are usually worked in pairs the number of stitches to be increased are halved and divided into the number of rows needed for the length. Allow some rows to be worked straight at the top of the sleeve after the last increase row.

Neckband

The neckband stitches are calculated by estimating that one stitch is picked up for every row at the side neck and adding those to the back and front neck stitches.

Getting Started

This is a very basic guide to compiling a simple pattern. Read it through carefully together with your preferred your preferred calculation table on pages 146-147 to make sure you understand everything. The formula may seem confusing at first, but it really is just simple maths. As you gain in confidence you will be able to experiment with different shapes and styles of garment.

Metric Sweater Calculations.

The following calculations are for the pattern for the simple sweater with dropped shoulders using the metric measurements.

Measurements: To fit 2-3 years.
Chest Measurements: 51-56cm.
Actual chest measures: 76cm.
Length: 38cm.
Sleeve length: 23cm.

Tension: 20 sts and 28 rows to 10cm square (2 sts and 2.8 rows to 1cm) over st st on 4mm (No. 8/US 6) needles.

Abbreviations: See page 158

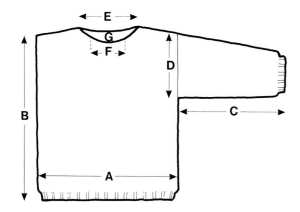

Width of back (A): 38cm.
Number of sts to be cast on: 38 x 2 = 76 plus 2 sts for sewing up = 78 sts.

Length of sweater (B) minus 5cm rib: 38cm - 5cm = 33cm.
Number of rows after rib: 33 x 2.8 = 92.4, round down to 92 rows.

Back neck width (E): 15cm.
Number of sts: 15 x 2 = 30 sts.

Shoulder sts: 78 - 30 (back neck width) = 48 sts.
Number of sts for each shoulder: 48 divided by 2 = 24 sts.

Front neck width (F): 8 cm.
Number of sts: 8 x 2 = 16 sts.

Neck shaping: 39 (half total front sts) – 8 (half front neck sts) = 31 sts.
Number of sts to be decreased for the neck: 31 – 24 (shoulder sts) = 7 sts.

Depth of neck (G): 7cm.
Number of rows: 7 x 2.8 = 19.6, round up to 20 rows.

Dec rows at neck edge: Divide the number of rows (20) by the number of stitches to be decreased (7) allowing a few rows straight after decreasing (13 or 6). You can dec 1 st on neck edge on first 7 rows, work straight. Or dec 1 st on neck edge on every alternate row, work straight.

Width of sleeve after rib: 23 cm.
Number of stitches after rib: 23 x 2 = 46 sts. Cast on for cuff 38 sts and inc 8 sts evenly on last row of rib.

Width of top of sleeve: 36 cm.
Number of stitches: 36 x 2 = 72 sts.
Number of stitches to be increased: 72 - 46 = 26 sts.
Number of paired increasings: 13.

Length of sleeve: (C) after 5cm rib: 23 - 5 = 18cm.
Number of rows: 18 x 2.8 = 50.4, round down to 50 rows.
Increase frequency: 50 divided by 13 = 3.8 Increase on every 3rd row.
No of rows worked straight at top of sleeve: 13 x 3 = 39 rows used for shaping.
50 - 39 = 11 rows to be worked straight.

Imperial Sweater Calculations.

The following calculations are for the pattern for the simple sweater with dropped shoulders using the imperial measurements.

Measurements: To fit 2-3 years.
Chest Measurements: 20-22in.
Actual chest measures: 30in.
Length: 15in.
Sleeve length: 9in.

Tension: 20 sts and 28 rows to 4in square (5 sts and 7 rows to 1in) over st st on US 6 (4mm/No. 8) needles.

Abbreviations: See page 158

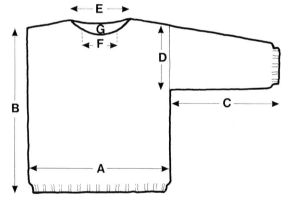

Width of back (A): 15in.
Number of sts to be cast on: 15 x 5 = 75, round up to even number, 76, plus 2 sts for sewing up = 78 sts.

Length of sweater (B) minus 1½ in rib:
15in - 1 ½ in = 13½ in.
Number of rows after rib: 13½ x 7 = 94½, round up to 96 rows.

Back neck width (E): 6 in.
Number of sts: 6 x 5 = 30 sts.

Shoulder sts: 78 – 30 (back neck width) = 48 sts.
Number of sts for each shoulder: 48 divided by 2 = 24 sts.

Front neck width (F): 3in.
Number of sts: 3 x 5 = 15 sts, round up to 16 sts.

Neck shaping: 39 (half total front sts) – 8 (half front neck sts) = 31 sts.
Number of sts to be decreased for the neck: 31 – 24 (shoulder sts) = 7 sts.

Depth of neck (G): 3in.
Number of rows: 3 x 7 = 21, round down to 20 rows.

Dec rows at neck edge: Divide the number of rows (20) by the number of stitches to be decreased (7) allowing a few rows straight after decreasing (13 or 6). You can dec 1 st on neck edge on first 7 rows, work straight. Or dec 1 st on neck edge on every alternate row, work straight.

Width of sleeve after rib: 9in.
Number of stitches after rib: 9 x 5 = 45, round up to 46 sts.
Cast on for cuff 38 sts and inc 8 sts evenly on last row of rib.

Width of top of sleeve: 14in.
Number of stitches: 14 x 5 = 70 sts.
Number of stitches to be increased: 70 – 46 = 24 sts.
Number of paired increasings: 12.

Length of sleeve: (C) after 1½ in rib:
9 – 1½ = 7½ in.
Number of rows: 17½ x 7 = 52½, round up to 54 rows.
Increase frequency: 54 divided by 12 = 4.
Increase after every 4th row.
No of rows worked straight at top of sleeve:
12 x 4 = 48 rows used for shaping.
54 – 48 = 6 rows to be worked straight.

CHAPTER NINE

Finishing Workshop

THIS IS ONE OF the most important workshops, as the ability to sew up properly using the most appropriate methods, and to rectify mistakes before you have completed the project, makes all the difference between an ordinary looking handknit and a professional one.

Some knitters of my acquaintance have admitted to me in weaker moments that they have bags of knitted pieces lying around waiting to be sewn up, but as they find this the most tedious part of the whole project they have put them away and moved on to something else.

For me however this can be the most rewarding part of the work, as not only do you get to wear the design at last, but there is a great deal of satisfaction gained in making the garment look as good as it possibly can.

I firmly believe that the craft of knitting deserves the best finishing, and that includes the wrong side of the fabric. Even the choice of buttons can be important as you may find that cheap, plastic ones can help to make the design look cheap, too.

Making Up

'Making up' is the term used to describe finishing your garment. Sloppy sewing up can ruin a beautifully knitted garment, but by using the methods shown here you can create virtually invisible seams. Check the ball band to see if there are any special pressing instructions you must follow first.

Joining A Side Seam On Stocking Stitch Fabric (Mattress Stitch)

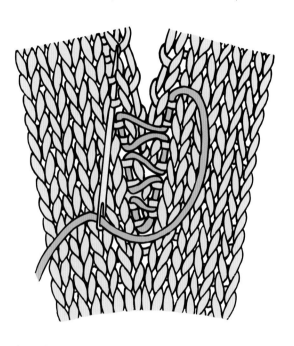

Right sides up, lay the pieces to be joined flat and edge to edge. Thread a blunt-pointed needle with yarn and attach the yarn to the back of one side. Bring the needle out to the front between the edge stitch and the second stitch in the first row. Insert the needle between the edge stitch and the second stitch in the first row on the opposite side. Pass the needle under the loops of one or two rows, then bring it back through to the front. Insert the needle into the hole that the last stitch came out of on the first side and pass it under the loops of one or two rows to emerge in the same place as on the opposite side.

Repeat this zigzag action, always taking the needle under the strands that correspond exactly to those on the other side, taking care not to miss any rows. After a few stitches pull up the yarn thus closing the seam. Make sure that the seam is at the same tension as the rest of the fabric.

Joining A Side Seam On Single Rib

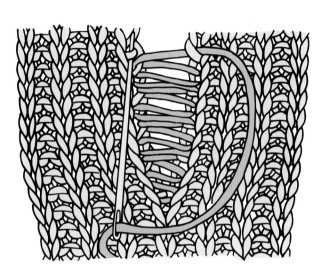

When joining two ribbed sections together, it is best to take in only half a stitch on either side, so that when the two pieces are drawn together one complete knit stitch in formed along the seam. Join the seam in the same way as for stocking stitch but pass the needle under the loop of one row at a time rather than two.

To join double rib use the same method, but take in a whole stitch, as with mattress stitch, for the least visible seam.

Joining Two Cast-off Edges

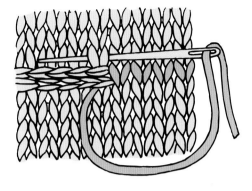 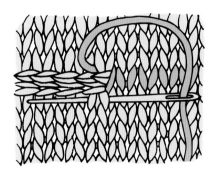

Two cast off edges can be joined together in a similar way as for a side seam. Bring the needle out in the centre of the first stitch below the casting off stitch on one side. Insert the needle in the centre of the first stitch on the opposite side and bring it out in the centre of the next stitch. Return to the first stitch and insert the needle in the centre of the first stitch, bring it out in the centre of the next stitch.

Joining A Side Seam On Reverse Stocking Stitch Fabric Or Background

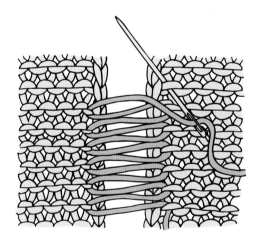

With the purl side of the fabric as the right side, join the seam in the same way as for stocking stitch but a better effect is achieved by passing the needle under the loop of one row at a time rather than the two rows as described for stocking stitch.

TIPS: SEAMS

Too often a well-knitted garment can be ruined and made to look unprofessional by rushing the final stages in your eagerness to sew up the design. Before you begin sewing up your garment you may need to block and press the all the pieces (see page 156).

The seams shown on these pages and on page 152 are suitable for a variety of situations on most garments, but the mattress stitch is the most versatile and, once perfected, can give a virtually invisible finish.

If possible, use the yarn that you have been knitting with for sewing up the seams, but if the garment is worked in a heavily textured yarn or a yarn that breaks easily, you will need to use a smooth yarn in a toning colour for sewing up.

If you have only used a backstitch or an oversewn seam before, try this method of sewing up and you will be surprised at how easy it is, and at how much better the finished seam looks. As mattress stitch is worked on the right side of the fabric it is invaluable for accurately matching stripes and bands of Fair Isle.

Backstitch Seam

This seam is only really suitable for lightweight yarns, double knitting at the heaviest. The seam is thicker and less elastic than mattress stitch and shows more definitely as a seam on the right side. It is also difficult to undo as each stitch has to be individually unpicked. Keep the seam allowance as narrow as possible – one stitch is the maximum and half a stitch will help minimise bulk.

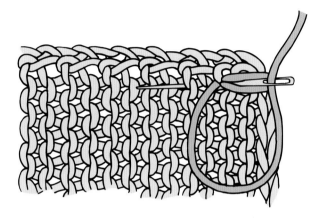

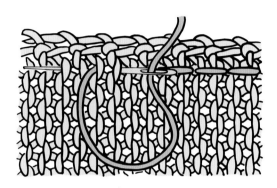

1 Pin the pieces right sides facing, matching row for row, and thread a blunt-ended needle. Take the needle round the two edges thus enclosing them with a strong stitch ending with the yarn at the front. Insert the needle into the work just behind where the last stitch came out and make a short stitch. Re-insert the needle where the previous stitch ended and make a stitch that is twice as long.

2 Put the needle back into the work where the previous stitch ended and make another stitch the same length as the one before. Repeat this to make a continuous line of stitches of equal length on the side of the work facing you.

Vertical/Sewn On Front Bands

These can be worked separately and sewn on afterwards. If the welt is also in rib, however, the band can be cast on and worked at the same time as the welt. When the welt is complete, the front band stitches are slipped onto a safety pin to be used later, while the remainder of the front is completed, usually on a larger needle. When the band is knitted up, an extra stitch should be cast on at the inside edge which will be taken into the seam.

Work the button side first, slightly stretching the band to fit front to neck shaping on round neck or to centre of back on V-neck, making notes of rows worked. Pin and sew in place. Work the other side to match, calculating where the buttonholes should be.

Picking Up Dropped Stitches

A dropped or incorrect stitch is a common mistake. Depending on the type of stitch dropped or when the mistake occurred you can pick up, unpick or unravel using the methods introduced next.

Picking Up A Knit Stitch On The Row Below

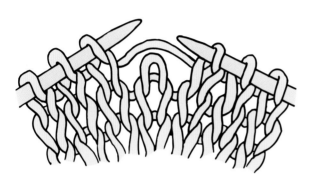

1 Try to pick up the dropped stitch as soon as possible or it will continue to 'unwind' further down the work.

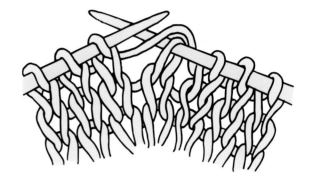

2 Working from front to back, pick up the stitch and the horizontal strand above it with the right-hand needle (the strand should be behind the stitch).

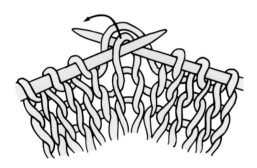

3 Insert the left-hand needle through the back of the stitch and lift it over the strand and off the needle as though casting off.

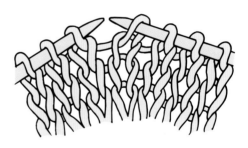

4 The stitch is made facing the wrong way. Insert the left-hand needle through the front of the stitch and slip it onto the needle. The stitch is then in the right position.

Picking Up A Purl Stitch On The Row Below

1 Try to pick up the dropped stitch as soon as possible or it will continue to 'unwind' further down the work.

2 Working from back to front, pick up the stitch and the horizontal strand above it with the right-hand needle (the strand should be in front of the stitch).

3 Insert the left-hand needle behind the strand and through the stitch. Lift the stitch.

4 With the right-hand needle, draw the strand through the lifted stitch so forming a stitch on the right-hand needle.

TIPS: CORRECTING MISTAKES

Even the most experienced knitters make mistakes from time to time, so don't panic as there are very few errors that cannot subsequently be put right.

Quite often you may not realise you have dropped a stitch until you get to a part in the pattern where you have to count the stitches. A stitch dropped a few rows below can be picked up and recreated on each row

(see page 155) as long as the work has not progressed too far. If it has, the stitches above the dropped stitch will be drawn too tightly across the back of the row to leave enough spare yarn to recreate the lost stitch. Under these circumstances it is much better to unravel the work (see page 155) to the point where the stitch was dropped and then reknit the unravelled rows.

Picking Up A Stitch Several Rows Below

The dropped stitch forms a ladder running down a number of rows and can be picked up with a crochet hook. Always work from the front – or knit side – of the fabric. Insert the hook into the free stitch from the front. With the hook pointing upwards, catch the first strand of the ladder from above and draw it through the stitch. Continue in this way until all the strands have been worked, then replace the stitch on the left-hand needle taking care not to twist it. If more than one stitch has been dropped, secure the others with a safety pin until you are ready to pick them up.

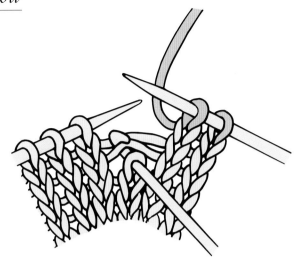

Unravelling

To go back stitch-by-stitch when a mistake has occurred more than a few rows down really is tedious and unnecessary. The quick way is to take the work off the needle and unravel it. Unravel the knitting to the row below the mistake, replace the stitches on the needle (ensuring that you have not twisted them) and continue knitting. With some yarns it may be difficult to replace the stitches neatly, so in these instances, unravel to the row above the mistake, replace the stitches on the needle and unpick one row.

On A Knit Row

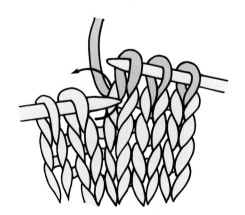

Keep yarn at the back and the knitting on right-hand needle. Insert left-hand needle from front to back through the centre of the first stitch below the stitch on the right-hand needle then withdraw the right-hand needle from the stitch and pull yarn free.

On A Purl Row

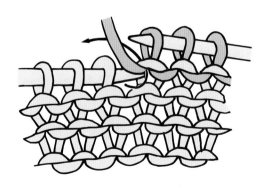

Unpick a purl row in the same way as a knit row, but keep the yarn at the front of the work.

Finishing Fabrics

Although not all garments are suitable for pressing, particularly if they are knitted in fancy or synthetic yarns, most will benefit from either blocking and pressing or damp finishing.

The importance of the finishing stages of a garment must never be overlooked. Too often a well-knitted garment can be spoilt by rushing the final stages, and the time and effort taken to knit the garment is wasted if the end result is unsatisfactory.

Most yarns which contain a high percentage of natural fibre can be pressed. However, there are some yarns which would be ruined by pressing, especially yarns made with a high percentage of acrylic or mohair. Always check the ball band for information on whether or not the yarn should be pressed – this should also tell you the heat setting of the iron and whether to use a dry or damp cloth. If the ball band states that the yarn should not be pressed, do follow this advice – your knitting can be damaged irreparably by a hot iron. Use the *Damp Finishing* method given opposite for these yarns. Pattern instructions may give more advice on pressing, but remember that the pressing requirements could be different if you have substituted another yarn.

Some types of knitting or parts of a garment are best left unpressed even if the yarn is suitable. These include ribbing, cable and texture patterns. Pressing may flatten the texture and blur the details, and can make ribbing loose its elasticity. Damp finishing is more suitable in these cases.

If in any doubt, always try pressing the tension swatch first to avoid spoiling the actual garment.

Blocking

This is the careful pinning out of separate pieces of knitting before pressing to ensure that they are the correct shape and measurements. This should always be done before joining seams. Blocking is very useful for smoothing out Fair Isle and colour motif work which often looks uneven, and for adjusting slightly the size or shape of a garment without reknitting it. For blocking and pressing you will need a flat, padded surface covered with a clean cloth, long dressmaker's pins with large, coloured heads, an iron and a pressing cloth.

1 Arrange the pieces of knitting wrong side up on the padded surface. Place pins at 2cm (1in) intervals, angled them through the very edge of the knitting into the padding, avoiding any ribbed sections.

2 Check that the measurements are correct and that the lines of stitches are straight in both the horizontal and vertical directions. Re-pin as necessary to achieve the correct size and shape, stretching or easing in slightly if required so that the outline forms a smooth edge between the pins.

Pressing

Each pinned-out section of knitting is pressed to give a smooth finish and help it to hold its shape. If there is no specific information on pressing the yarn on the ball band use the following as a general guide. Wool, cotton, linen and other natural yarns: using a damp cloth, steam thoroughly without allowing the iron to rest on the work.

Synthetics: do not press 100% synthetic yarns. For yarns that are a mixture (those containing some natural fibres), use a cool iron over a dry cloth.

1 Cover the pinned-out pieces with a damp or dry cloth depending on the yarn. Check that the iron is the correct heat, then press evenly and lightly, lifting the iron up and down to avoid dragging the knitted material underneath. Do not press ribbed edges.

2 After pressing, remove a few pins. If the edge stays flat, take out all the pins and leave the knitting to dry completely before removing it from the flat surface. If the edge curls when a few pins are removed, re-pin it and leave it to dry with the pins in position.

3 After joining the completed pieces of knitting (see pages 150–152), press the seams lightly on the wrong side using the same method as before, although they will not require pinning.

Damp Finishing

This method of finishing is suitable for fluffy and synthetic yarns as well as textured patterns – all of which can be damaged by pressing.

1 Lay the pieces on a damp, and colourfast, towel then roll them up together and leave for about an hour to allow the knitting to absorb moisture from the towel. Unwrap, lay the damp towel on a flat surface and place the pieces on top of it.

2 Ease the pieces into shape and pin as explained in steps 1 and 2 of 'Blocking'. Lay another damp towel or tea-towel over the top, pat all over firmly to establish contact and leave until dry.

Caring For Knitwear

Now that all your time and effort have been rewarded by seeing your hand knit design completed, you will want to make sure that it keeps looking good for as long as possible. The following tips are guidelines to prevent your knits looking tired and unloved, but remember that the way you wear them can make a difference too. Too much tugging and stretching can pull welts out of shape.

Handmade garments are not always as resilient as ready-made garments, they are more likely to stretch out of shape or shrink if handled incorrectly. Some yarns now specify on the ball band that they can be machine washed on a specific cycle, and some can even be tumble dried.

If you are unsure about the washing qualities of a yarn use your tension swatch as a test for shrinkage and colour fastness.

Handwashing

One of the main problems associated with washing wool and wool mix fibres is shrinkage, often coupled with a harsh, matted appearance. Treat your handknits gently by using lukewarm water and a mild soap washing agent, preferably a liquid.

Never leave a knitted garment to soak, squeeze it to loosen the dirt, and then let the water out of the basin. Do not lift the garment out at this stage as the weight of the water will pull it out of shape. Gently squeeze out as much water as possible before running one or two rinses. Squeeze the last rinse water out and then supporting the weight lay the garment on a colourfast towel and roll it up quite loosely. Transfer to a dry towel and reshape to the correct measurements. (Some fibres may be spun on a short, gentle cycle, and cotton benefits from being spun as retained moisture may distort the garment.)

Leave to dry naturally away from direct sunlight or a source of heat, such as a radiator.

Machine Washing

Follow the washing guide lines on the ball band or use the method you consider suitable for the yarn. If you wish, the garment can be placed in a pillow case to prevent stretching. Stick to the recommended temperature – the water must not be hotter .

Read the symbols on the ball band and match them to the programme on your washing machine. At the end of the cycle remove it as soon as possible from the machine or it may crease. Lay it on a towel, reshape and allow to dry naturally.

If in doubt, handwash!

Dry Cleaning

Some yarns state the dry cleaning is recommended. Show the ball band when you take it in and ensure that the garment isn't put on a hanger or pressed.

Storing

Never keep garments on a hanger – heavy knits will drop or the hanger may come through the shoulders. If you want to store the garment for any length of time, wash or dry clean it first.

Basic Information

Standard Abbreviations

These are abbreviations for instructions, techniques and stitch libraries illustrated in this book.

alt = alternate: **beg** = begin(ning); **cont** = continue; **dec** = decreas(e)ing; **foll** = following; **inc** = increas(e)ing; **k** = knit; **m1** = make one; **patt** = pattern; **p** = purl; **psso** = pass slipped st over; **rem** = remain(ing); **rep** = repeat; **skpo** = sl 1, k1, pass slipped st over; **sl** = slip; **st(s)** = stitch(es); **st st** = stocking stitch; **tbl** = through back of loop(s); **tog** = together; **yb** = yarn back; **yf** = yarn forward; **yon** = yarn over needle; **yrn** = yarn round needle.

Special Abbreviations For Aran Stitch Library

C2F = slip next st onto cable needle and leave at front of work, k1, then k1 from cable needle.
C2B = slip next st onto cable needle and leave at back of work, k1, then k1 from cable needle.
C3F = slip next 2 sts onto cable needle and leave at front of work, k1, then k2 from cable needle.
C3B = slip next st onto cable needle and leave at back of work, k2, then k1 from cable needle.
C4F = slip next 2 sts onto cable needle and leave at front of work, k2, then k2 from cable needle.
C4B = slip next 2 sts onto cable needle and leave at back of work, k2, then k2 from cable needle.
C6F = slip next 3 sts onto cable needle and leave at front of work, k3, then k3 from cable needle.
C6B = slip next 3 sts onto cable needle and leave at back of work, k3, then k3 from cable needle.
C2FW = slip next st onto cable needle and leave at front of work, p1, then p1 from cable needle.
C2BW = slip next st onto cable needle and leave at back of work, p1, then p1 from cable needle.
Cr2R = slip next st onto cable needle and leave at back of work, k1, then p1 from cable needle.
Cr2L = slip next st onto cable needle and leave at front of work, p1, then k1 from cable needle.
Cr3R = slip next st onto cable needle and leave at back of work, k2, then p1 from cable needle.
Cr3L = slip next 2 sts onto cable needle and leave at front of work, p1, then k2 from cable needle.

Cr4R = slip next 2 sts onto cable needle and leave at back of work, k2, then k1, p1 from cable needle.
Cr4L = slip next 2 sts onto cable needle and leave at front of work, k1, p1, then k2 from cable needle.
Cr4B = slip next 2 sts onto cable needle and leave at back of work, k2, then p2 from cable needle.
Cr4F = slip next 2 sts onto cable needle and leave at front of work, p2, then k2 from cable needle.
Cr5R = slip next 2 sts onto cable needle and leave at back of work, k3, then p2 from cable needle.
Cr5L = slip next 3 sts onto cable needle and leave at front of work, p2, then k3 from cable needle.
Tw2L = slip next st onto cable needle and leave at front of work, p1, then k1 tbl from cable needle.
Tw2R = slip next st onto cable needle and leave at back of work, k1 tbl, then p1 from cable needle.
Tw2LW = slip next st onto cable needle and leave at front of work, p1 tbl, then k1 from cable needle.
Tw2RW = slip next st onto cable needle and leave at back of work, k1, then p1 tbl from cable needle.

Yarn Weights

If you want to substitute a yarn, choose one of the same type and weight as that recommended. The amount needed is determined by metres/yards rather than by ounces/grams. Remember to always test a substitute yarn to see if it will achieve the correct tension.

The following descriptions of various Rowan yarns are a guide to the yarn type and weight.

4-ply Cotton: a light-weight 100% cotton yarn, approx. 170m/186yd per 50g/1¾oz ball.
Cotton Glace: a lightweight 100% cotton yarn, approx. 112m/123yd per 50g/1¾oz ball.
Designer DK Wool: a double-knitting-weight 100% wool yarn, approx. 115m/125yd per 50g/1¾oz ball.
DK Handknit Cotton: a medium-weight 100% cotton yarn, approx. 85m/90yd per 50g/1¾oz ball.
DK Tweed: a double-knitting-weight 100% wool yarn, approx. 110m/120yd per 50g/1¾oz ball.
Magpie: Aran weight 100% wool yarn, approx. 140m/154yd per 100g/3½oz hank.
Magpie Aran and **Tweed:** Aran-weight 100% wool yarn, approx. 150m/164yd per 100g/3½oz hank.

Stockists / Distributors

Debbie Bliss's shop is at the following address:
Debbie Bliss, 365 St John Street, London
EC1V 4LB. Tel: 0171 833 8255.
For overseas stockists and mail-order information
for Rowan yarns please contact:
Canada: Diamond Yarn, 9697 St Laurent, Montreal,
Quebec, H3L 2N1. Tel: 514 388 6188.
Diamond Yarn, 1450 Lodestar, Unit 4, Toronto,
Ontario, M3J 3C1. Tel: 416 636 1212.
Denmark: Ruzicka, Hydesbyvej 27, DK 4990
Sakakoing. Tel: 54 70 78 04.
France: Elle Tricot, 52 Rue Principale, 67300
Schiltigheim. Tel: 88 62 65 31.
Germany: Wolle & Design, Wlofshovener Strasse
76, 52428 Julich-Stetternich. Tel: 02461/54735.
Holland: Henk & Henriette Beukers, Dorpsstraat 9,
NL 5327 AR Hurwenen. Tel: 0418 661764.

Hong Kong: East Unity Company Ltd, Rm 902,
Block A, Kailey Industrial Centre, 12 Fung Yip
Street, Chair Wan. Tel: 852 2869 7110.
Italy: Victoriana, Via Fratelli Pioli 14, Rivioli, (TO).
Tel: 011 95 32 142.
Japan: Diakeito Co Ltd, 2-3-11 Senba-Higashi,
Minoh City, Osaka 562. Tel: 0727 27 6604.
Norway: Eureka, PO Box 357, N 1401 Ski.
Tel: 64 86 55 40.
Sweden: Wincent, Sveavagen 94, 113 50
Stockholm. Tel: 08673 70 60.
UK: Rowan Yarns, Green Mill Lane, Holmfirth,
West Yorkshire HD7 1RW. Tel: 01484 681881.
USA: Westminster Fibers Inc., 5 Northern
Boulevard, Amherst, New Hampshire 03031.
Tel: 603 886 5041/5043.
E-mail: WFIBERATAOL.COM

Acknowledgements

I am very grateful to the following knitters for their great skill: Pat Church, Connie Critchell, Penny Hill, Shirley Kennet, Masie Lawrence and Frances Wallace.

I would like to thank Sandra Lane and Sandra Lousada for their beautiful photography and Sammie Bell for her perfect styling.

This book would not have been possible without the following people: Cindy Richards for creating and inspiring the project. Kate Haxell, a fantastic editor, who as a new knitter asked all the right questions. Tina Egleton, whose expertise and technical knowledge were invaluable. A special thank you to Heather Jeeves, a wonderful agent.

Index